# The
# Entrepreneur
# Bridge:

## How to Overcome the 7 Top Barriers to Business Success

### W. GLEN THOMPSON

Published by Stimulus Press, an imprint of Glen International LLC
2951 Marina Bay Dr., Ste. 130-255, League City, Texas, 77573
Printed in the United States of America

Publisher's Cataloging-In-Publication Data
(Prepared by The Donohue Group, Inc.)

Thompson, W. Glen.

The entrepreneur bridge : how to overcome the 7 top barriers to business success / W. Glen Thompson. -- 1st ed.

p. ; cm.

Issued also as an eBook.

Includes bibliographical references.

ISBN: 978-0-9888436-0-8 (trade paper)

1. Entrepreneurship. 2. New business enterprises. 3. Success in business. I. Title.

HD62.5 .T46 2013

658.11

eBook ISBN: 978-0-9888436-1-5

A catalog record for the eBook edition is available at OCLC and SkyRiver for the use of their member libraries.

This publication is designed to provide general information on a particular subject or subjects and is not an exhaustive treatment of such subjects. It is sold with the understanding that the publisher and author does not intend it to constitute legal, financial, consulting or any other professional advice or services. If legal advice or expert assistance is required, and before making any decision or taking any action that might affect your finances or business, the services of a competent professional advisor should be sought.

Certain product or service names mentioned may be the trademarks or registered trademarks of Glen International LLC. Any other product or service names mentioned are the trademarks or registered trademarks of their respective owners and are mentioned for identification purposes only.

# CONTENTS

# ACKNOWLEDGMENTS

First of all, grateful thanks to my wife Emma, for all your continuous love and support. Also to my Mother, for your love and encouragement that made me a believer in my Faith and in myself.

To my friends, colleagues, mentors, and clients, thanks for encouraging me along my journey.

Thanks to Eric Brantner and Rob Bignell for developmental and copy editing services.

Thanks, also, to Ann Mauren and Amanda L. Matthews of AM Design Studios for book design services.

Finally and importantly, to entrepreneurs and those that support entrepreneurialism, you are the most interesting people in the world.

# 1

## INTRODUCTION TO THE JOURNEY

It's not a straight line, and not a sudden decision. It's filled with twists and turns, highs and lows, barriers and bridges over them. It's a journey for entrepreneurs. A path of learning, experiences, and then realizations about one's self leading to an entrepreneurial destination.

It's a rewarding journey. What kind of rewards? Part of it are the challenges and excitement along the way in starting your own business; then the education and learning; independence of doing it for yourself; freedom and potential for wealth. The rewards are various, but always meaningful and intense.

In my entrepreneurial journey thus far, much of it has been typical of entrepreneurs, such as my experience background and my ventures being an outgrowth of that. Or my willingness to walk off the beaten path and take on risk. I also came from humble beginnings as many do. I grew up, by some people's standards, as a poor farm boy in rural Louisiana, but I didn't know I was poor. I learned many values back then which were enriching to my life, helping me go from the farm yard to the board room, and from herding steers to steering businesses.

Then there are the unpredictable surprises in the journey, such as the day I went from business consulting to being a cancer patient. It was a turn taking me to where I was a rediscovering soul of what I believe and what inspires me, and helped me to refocus on what's most important to me. I realized anew we only have a certain amount of time on this earth, and we should not put off important goals. Instead, we should invest in ourselves and in others right now. I think nothing is more rewarding than helping people reach their goals of success.

This is my purpose in writing my books and as founder of my companies, which are committed to providing business information and business coaching enabling the success of entrepreneurs and businesses. Through the two decades of my entrepreneurial business journey thus far, I've been privileged to work with some great companies and customers. I've observed and experienced their challenges and successes. It fuels my passion for entrepreneurs and business to see them reach the dream goals of their entrepreneurial journey.

You're reading this because of your own journey as an entrepreneur. Where you are in that journey, could be that you want to be an entrepreneur and start your own business, or perhaps you have tried starting a business without success, or have had some success and want more. Wherever you are in your journey, you are seeking answers for important questions: Is now a good time to start a business? If I failed should I try again? What are the major barriers for entrepreneurs? How do I overcome the challenges? What are the characteristics of a successful entrepreneur? Is there a roadmap that I can follow to help me? This book will help you answer such questions.

There has never been a better time to be an entrepreneur and start a business; never a better time to join the ranks of the expanding entrepreneurial economy and reach for the achievement, independence, and satisfaction of entrepreneurialism. How so? Because there has never been such availability and access to low-cost, high-value technology, marketing and information. This is a great equalizer that truly assists anyone considering entrepreneurship in starting a business at a low cost and with real opportunity for success.

There is also tremendous support and information available to an individual in starting a business today from specialized organizations to experienced advisors sharing methods, templates and advice to enable the entrepreneur. Not only is this available at reasonable cost but great amounts of it are free. Also, you will be amazed at facts I will share about how successful companies have started in the past during recessions or worse.

But it's not easy. There are challenges for every individual as an entrepreneur. I grew up in the countryside near a small town on a river. A state highway came through the town and crossed the river, back then on a steel and concrete bridge constructed in the 1930s. The bridges constructed in that time were much lower and closer to the water than the bridges with the main spans and approaches built today. In the years that there would be heavy spring rains, the river would rise significantly, and there would be a lot of runoff from the woods and farms that would enter it.

I remember as a very young child riding in the car with my mother and crossing that bridge. That year, the water level was extremely high. I looked down at the river and was surprised by how large, wide, and high it was. The current was boiling and swirling as the water rushed under the bridge with this refuse being swept away. It looked very scary to a little boy who was seeing it so close for the first time.

After that, I began to have a recurring dream. Actually, it was a recurring nightmare. In this nightmare, I was climbing off that bridge and hanging onto the side. Then, I let go and fell backwards off the bridge, screaming as I went down toward the water below. I would always wake up just before I hit the water and find myself sitting in bed with this horrible feeling of fear inside me. Later, I always wondered what would have happened in that dream if I didn't wake up just before I hit the water.

In some ways, my dream is very much like the journey entrepreneurs face. In traveling down the entrepreneur's road, you'll find yourself peering into the swirling whirlpools of troubling challenges. There will be barriers blocking your path as you work your way toward success. These barriers and their turbulent situations will loom large and are the cause of thousands of failed entrepreneurs letting go of the bridge and abandoning their dreams. Unfortunately, many are swept away from the pathway to success by the troubles they encounter which cause fear and not focusing on the bridge. If only they had been aware of what they would face and how they could prepare to cross over it. My goal is to make you aware of the challenges entrepreneurs can face and that you can prepare to bridge over them.

In fact, I will share with you seven top barriers entrepreneurs encounter. These seven are not just from opinions or academic studies, but come from the actual experience and observations of hundreds of entrepreneurs. As we look at each of these top barriers to success for entrepreneurs, I will provide experiences, research, and case examples which provide attitudes and approaches for overcoming them.

Entrepreneurial success is about how well you build a bridge to get over the barriers you encounter when starting and building a business. This is why I share story after story of entrepreneurs who are finding a way in their struggles to build a bridge over these top barriers. I will also share with you what are the nine competencies and their characteristics of a successful entrepreneur. So that you know what strengths you may have to leverage and weaknesses to strengthen. In addition and more importantly, I will share with you a roadmap with five steps that accelerates entrepreneurs with a system of solid methods, templates, and guidance that can assist the average person in the entrepreneurial journey down a roadmap to success.

Entrepreneurs are fascinating. They are the most interesting people in the world. How could they not be? This group will take a little money and big risks because they see an opportunity and with creativity and commitment develop a business. How do they do it? By discovering and following their passion and daring to leave the shadows of mediocrity. With a life with such feeling and excitement, it could be life at its finest. You can call it The American Dream or whatever else you want to call it, but it's real and it can be yours. You just have to want it.

But don't listen to the negative voices. As Steve Jobs, co-founder of Apple and Pixar said, "Don't let the noise of other's opinions drown out your own inner voice. And most important, have the courage to follow your heart and intuition. They somehow already know what you truly want to become." There is a long history of many voices with misinformation, opinions and conclusions out there around entrepreneurs. Much of it is mythological, boringly academic, or narrowly focused on inward-centered, niche groups, debating from what is the definition of an entrepreneur or whether there is becoming more or less of them to which techniques are valid. So much better I think if there is just blended, balanced information provided that's applicable for those interested from the rest of us in starting a business successfully. If starting a business calls to you, don't be distracted from listening to your passion. It could be a regret.

In this book, a journey awaits you. It is one with dangers to prepare for, insights to learn, and bridges to build over your barriers. It includes daring entrepreneurial stories full of encouragement, facts from research and case studies, and if it suits you, the opportunity to find the best use of yourself in reaching your dreams as an entrepreneur.

If you think you're ready to further explore your journey as an entrepreneur success story, I want to share in your success with you, by providing you information, motivation, and methods that work and will help you bridge the barriers to success.

W. Glen Thompson

*www.successfulentrepreneuradvisor.com*

# 2

## A GREAT TIME TO BE AN ENTREPRENEUR

There has never been a better time than right now for you to become an entrepreneur.

Some of you might doubt this declaration, and understandably so. After all, we're still in what has been dubbed the "Great Recession." Unemployment is high, the government is a mess with its own fiscal cliff looming, and financial lenders are tighter with loan approvals than ever before. The economic environment hasn't been getting any better and there are not any forecasts out there for it to improve anytime soon. The Federal Reserve, the central banking system of the United States, recently reduced its growth forecast for the rest of this year and into the next. The Fed has also reported there has been a huge drop of 40% in average household wealth.

The bust in housing is slow to recover from its impacts with a high number of bankruptcies while many of those still in their homes are upside down with their mortgage. A record number of Americans live on food stamps, every 1-in-7. These are the virtual bread lines you don't see similar to the 1930's since these benefits are paid with debit cards. Then there is the advertised unemployment rate of nearly 8% as compared to the real unemployment rate of 15%, which factors in those who are working only part-time or have given up on getting a job and dropped out altogether.

Many financial experts are concerned that the country is headed for a "double-dip" recession and even others go so far as to call this economic malaise we are in a "modern day depression."

In this environment, with some actually afraid they could retire below the poverty line, more and more people are realizing they must be self-reliant and take their future into their own hands. They recognize with the sum of all their experience, skills, and attitudes, they are a valuable human asset; and as such, are their own greatest resource they can leverage in generating income.

**Recessions Breed Entrepreneurs**

How could it be possible that in the midst of challenging economic times lies the greatest opportunity in our lifetimes for becoming an entrepreneur?

The Kauffman Foundation of Entrepreneurship, a private, nonpartisan foundation that through its research and other initiatives supports entrepreneurship and innovation, shows an upward trend in entrepreneurship. The March 2011 release of the Kauffman Index of Entrepreneurial Activity showed that 2010 had the highest rates of entrepreneur activity in 15 years. Think of it…during the Great Recession, more Americans were becoming entrepreneurs than at any time in the past 15 years. That includes some pretty great economic years during the Internet boom of the 1990s. Then with the March 2012 release

Kauffman reported for 2011 that although there was a slight dip while still in the aftershocks of the Great Recession, that entrepreneurship was still alive and well with approximately 543,000 new businesses created each month during the year. This keeping the rate of entrepreneur activity remaining more than 5 percent higher than before the recession started. Kauffman reports this is still among the highest levels of entrepreneurship over the past 16 years.

Kauffman's Facts on Entrepreneurship and the Economy mentions the Start-Up Phenomenon where well-over half of the companies on the 2009 *Fortune* 500 list and just under half of those on the 2008 *Inc.* 500 list began during a recession or bear market. Perhaps you would recognize some of these company names founded during a recession or bear market: 3M, Apple, CNN, Chevron, Dave and Buster's, Disney, Enterprise Rent-A-Car, Genentech, GE, IBM, Microsoft, Quiznos, Scottrade, Whole Foods...shall I go on?

Another report from Kauffman states that even the Great Depression, lasting from late 1929 to early 1933, with lingering effects long after that and followed by a recession in 1937-1938, wouldn't indicate a particularly great time to start a company. Yet they say that during this decade, one filled with economic turmoil, an above-average number of Fortune 500 Companies were founded.

Back then, governmental organizations were created to support the economy, like the Civilian Conservation Corps (CCC) – affectionately known as the CC Camps, the Reconstruction Finance Corporation which over time evolved into the Small Business Administration (SBA), and the Federal Housing Administration (FHA) that was designed to combat the housing crisis of the Great Depression.

I have a lot of family who lived through the Great Depression—parents, aunts and uncles, grandparents, and great uncles and aunts. From their stories I know they did what they could and had to do by utilizing what resources and skills they had available to make a living. They shared...they helped one another...they were clever...and most of all, they worked hard. Simply put, they were entrepreneurial. It was the only way they could keep their heads above water.

Amongst some of my folks, one had a carpentry business, another a painting business, and another who had a farm and worked a job on the side, which was pretty common back then.

I heard stories about every community having an enterprising person who would start a small country store since few people had transportation to go to a town. Those little stores didn't carry a lot of items, but if you needed some basic food item or feed for the animals, you could usually get something there to make do and get by.

The people who ran them were very frugal and managed to obtain the property to locate the store on, and they would also farm the land for vegetables along with running the store. It was tough work that included long, hard hours, but they were successful entrepreneurs until automobiles became more affordable in the 1940s, enabling the average person to travel into town. A lot of those businesses slowly died out, or they adapted.

I recall the story told by my mom about a rolling grocery store that came through their community. The man used an old school bus as his transportation, delivering and selling groceries to folks that he brought in from the nearest town. Later on, he opened a thriving variety store in a building in that town. He was a successful entrepreneur who started with nothing more than an old bus, a great idea, and a passion to succeed.

Even the original school buses that transported the children to school were owned by entrepreneurs then. For years, they were privately operated by individuals who contracted with the parish school board. My folks have told me about their first memories of a school bus. It had wooden sides and cloth flaps to cover the windows. They said it was unbearably cold in the winter and miserably hot in the summer, but it still sure beat walking to school.

## America's Entrepreneurial Spirit Still Lives

Don't underestimate the spirit of America and its people. There is another revival of entrepreneurialism happening that continues our legacy, where people of all stripes and levels are picking themselves up by their bootstraps and blazing their own trails as entrepreneurs to make a living—and some even growing wealth. They still have that dream burning deep inside, and they're committed to turning it into a reality.

Most Americans do believe in the importance of entrepreneurs. In another recent survey also conducted by the Kauffman Foundation, 57% of respondents agreed that becoming an entrepreneur is an opportunity available to most Americans. Additionally, a whopping 70% agreed that the success and health of our economy depends on the success of entrepreneurs. By the way, this survey was conducted when the economic crisis was at its very worst in September 2008.

Recently, I was watching CNN's Piers Morgan interviewing Suze Orman, a personal finance expert and TV personality. At one point, Morgan asked Orman what could be done to fix the political and economic mess facing our country. Part of Orman's response was that people are going to have to become entrepreneurial. She said that Americans are going to have to become their own bosses and that the day of working for a corporation, getting a pension after 30 years, and receiving health benefits are gone.

I found myself wanting to stand up from the couch and give Suze Orman a standing ovation. She's right; if you really want to achieve financial and personal security, be your own boss. Don't wait for the next politician to win office, crossing your fingers that their promises will come to fruition. Don't wait on some government program to bail you out. Be an entrepreneur; create your own future of success.

Entrepreneurs and small businesses are an engine of growth for America and the global economy. Entrepreneurship is essential for economic development, and entrepreneurs play an important role in the development of successful economies. They always have and always will.

I also believe that if we ever want to truly rebound from the Great Recession, Americans must support entrepreneurialism, just as those who lived before us did during the Great Depression. Once again, it's time for us to come together, pull ourselves up by the bootstraps, and find creative ways to use our skills and resources to grow successful businesses that support the country, the world, and each other.

We need a renaissance of support and enablement for American Entrepreneurialism where companies want to build and expand in the USA and government begins to cooperate and puts in place policies and programs that promote entrepreneurialism. It's like accomplished economist Brian Wesbury said recently on Bloomberg Business TV, "We need an environment that fosters and supports entrepreneurialism…an environment where entrepreneurs can grow business and grow the American economy."

Business models sustained by a good business environment, promoted by good government policy, and supported by established companies providing capital and partnering with entrepreneurs—that's what this country needs.

I think Americans are ready and pacing with great ideas and businesses that will help once again create and propagate what made America great. They just need an opening, a chance and a way, a bridge over the challenges. Those who can support it and enable it with knowledge, experience, methods, capital, and policy should do so and with new enthusiasm.

## Entrepreneurs Are Everywhere You Look

The word "entrepreneur" was originally derived from the French word *enterprendre*, which means "to undertake." Sixteenth century Frenchmen who led military expeditions were referred to as "entrepreneurs." Later on, in the 18th century, the term "entrepreneur" was applied to business by the French economist Cantillon. Afterward, it was further popularized by the economist, Jean-Baptiste Say, who used the term to refer to individuals who create value in an economy as an organizer of a business. British economist John Stuart Mill took this definition a little further when he used the word in his classic economics textbook *The Principles of Political Economy* to describe someone who assumes both the risk and management of a business.

So, entrepreneurs are people who organize and manage an enterprise, especially a business, with considerable initiative and risk, hoping to make money.

When you think of it in these terms, you begin to realize that entrepreneurs are everywhere you look. I see them all around me today. I know them. I've hired them and worked with them.

I see the laid off worker and the immigrant citizen who have started their landscape companies with their used trucks, trailers, lawnmowers, and trimmers, working hard to make a living for their families.

I see the corporate professional who leaves a good job and career to pursue a dream by starting a non-profit organization that helps underprivileged kids gain vital business skills that put them on the path to becoming successful entrepreneurs.

I see the single mother with three small children who has no other choice but to pull herself up by the bootstraps to provide for her family. With determination and hard work, she claws her way up from a trainee to becoming a successful business manager who starts three offices, raises the business revenues into the millions, and now makes a six-figure income.

I see the IT worker who took the chance to start his own company as a consultant and now makes a handsome six figure income.

I see the intrapreneur, the person who is the entrepreneur within a larger organization, focusing on innovation, creativity, and transforming the business from within by implementing new processes and technology.

Now think about it. You probably see entrepreneurs in your life also. And they're only continuing to grow in numbers during these tough economic times.

I truly believe that there has never been a better time to be an entrepreneur than right at this very moment. The opportunity is great, and the rewards that come with being an entrepreneur are even greater.

What kind of rewards am I talking about?

- **Independence**—One of the most common reasons people decide to become entrepreneurs is because they don't want to work for someone else.

They don't want to be another follower; they want to be the one calling the shots. The independence you get as an entrepreneur is so very rewarding.

- **Pride from your achievements**—Even the smallest achievements (like landing your first customer) can be so rewarding for an entrepreneur. When you see all of your hard work starting to pay off as you reach your goals, you'll get a feeling of pride that picks you up and motivates you to work even harder.

- **Wealth**—It's the American Dream—start your own business and make lots of money. While you might not get rich overnight, you have the opportunity to attain wealth if you have a great plan, work hard, and stick with it when times get tough. Will you be the next Mark Cuban? Probably not, but you certainly have the opportunity to make a better life for yourself and your family.

- **Freedom**—As an entrepreneur, you have complete freedom from the 9-5 rat race. I love the flexibility that comes with this lifestyle. Sure, you have to work hard, and you'll often find yourself bone tired, but you won't be chained to a desk working for someone else. And if you want to occasionally take a day off to go to the beach with your family, who's going to stop you? You're the boss!

## Why Now is the Best Time for Entrepreneurs

Imagine for a moment…

…if you could start a business without needing much money; the tools and technology you need for running your business are already there for you at little to no cost; and there are people available to support you in growing your business. The only thing that's needed is the main ingredient: YOU! Your unique knowledge, skills, experience, commitment, and hard work.

You'd consider starting your own business if that was the case, right? Guess what—that *is* the case! What are you waiting for?

That's right. Today, you have access to more resources that are higher quality and lower priced than ever before. It's the perfect recipe for entrepreneurial success.

This expanding shift to this entrepreneurial economy is enabled by the availability of low-cost, high-value technology. It's never been easier and cheaper for someone to setup their own business office in their home. All the necessary equipment, like computers, printers, office phones, smart phones, software, and more, has become increasingly affordable. It's possible to look bigger, do more, and be more efficient and professional with less cost.

No-cost to low-cost applications that can be used for business are available online for anyone with an Internet connection. Things like email, calendars, project management tools, conference calling applications, social media (such as LinkedIn, Facebook, Twitter and YouTube) for marketing, and a host of other basic business applications are all there for you.

Above all else, there is the availability of information on the Internet, much of it free, where any person can learn how to start and grow a business.

There are also experienced business people and organizations that are committed to helping entrepreneurs get their businesses off the ground successfully. Some of them offer this support for free. Such an example would be SCORE, a nonprofit association dedicated to educating entrepreneurs and helping small businesses start, grow, and succeed. They offer small business entrepreneurs confidential counseling at no charge.

The Internet is also a great place to find affordable labor resources, from freelance web designers to marketers to virtual assistants, and so much more.

And for serious entrepreneurs, there are experienced business advisors, such as myself and others, that can accelerate you along your journey to success with motivation and proven methods that can save you effort, time, and money.

In each chapter of this book, you will also find tips, advice, statistics, and inspirational stories that will help you create a bridge over obstacles you may face on your journey to an entrepreneur's success.

What a perfect setup for the entrepreneur! What a great time it is to start or grow a business!

# 3

## ENTREPRENEUR BRIDGE OVER THE 7 TOP BARRIERS TO SUCCESS

They say that nothing worth having comes easy, and when it comes to being a successful entrepreneur, this is especially true. Yes, this is the best time ever to be an entrepreneur, but just because opportunity abounds doesn't mean that success is going to be handed to you.

Every entrepreneur faces challenges. That laid-off worker and the immigrant citizen with the landscaping companies, they have to struggle with building enough capital to buy new equipment or maintain their current equipment so that there are no missed working days. The corporate professional who left a good job to start a non-profit organization struggled mightily with becoming willing to accept the risks of leaving a secure, stable job and working to achieve a dream. The single mother who climbed the ladder to success constantly fights to find a balance between her work and home life so to meet the needs of the business and the needs of her children.

The stories of successful entrepreneurs are replete with examples of how they first had to overcome situational barriers to their success. For example, Burt Shavitz (lived in an 8'x8' cabin) sold honey from the back of his pickup truck and Roxanne Quimby (camped in a one room tent with kids) was an out-of-work waitress trying to make a living at flea markets and yard sales when they met. After she found a 19th-century book of homemade personal-care recipes, together they made and sold home-made beeswax lip balms and hand salves at local craft fairs. Their company, Burt's Bees, eventually went on to sell more than 100 skin- and hair-care items with sales topping over a quarter billion and then Clorox paid almost a billion to buy the company. Keep reading—I will share many more overcoming entrepreneur stories in this book.

The truth is there will be barriers to success for every entrepreneur. I have studied many entrepreneur case studies and invariably each one met barriers they had to overcome prior to their success. These barriers vary from one entrepreneur to the next, depending on their backgrounds, abilities, personalities, industry, and a host of other factors, but without a doubt, they will be there. If you want to be successful, you're going to have to face these barriers head on and find a way to overcome them.

## 7 Top Barriers to Entrepreneurial Success

A research report by the Kauffman Foundation of Entrepreneurship, *The Anatomy of an Entrepreneur: Making of a Successful Entrepreneur*, provided research that was based on a survey of 549 company founders in a variety of industries, and it explored their insights into the barriers faced by new entrepreneurs.

All told, these 549 business owners identified seven main barriers to an entrepreneur's success. These were not all that were identified but were commonly the seven top barriers.

Some of these barriers scare people away from ever taking the leap to become an entrepreneur; others appear later on and threaten to destroy businesses in different stages of their development.

The good news is that there are bridges you can build to overcome each of these barriers, but before we discuss that, let's identify briefly these seven top barriers to entrepreneurial success.

## 1. Lack of willingness or ability to take risks

There's a reason becoming an entrepreneur is often referred to as "taking the leap." For many, it's a very scary proposition to take such risk and start up a business. In fact, the Kauffman study found that 98 percent of respondents felt that a lack of willingness or ability to take risks was an important barrier to entrepreneurship. Simply put, many view entrepreneurship as a risky endeavor that they just aren't willing to undertake.

Think about everything you have to risk to become an entrepreneur. You may have to give up your job. If you go out on your own and fail, that stable job probably won't be waiting for you if you want to go back. Then there's the money. Many entrepreneurs use their own savings to start a business. It's certainly a gamble, and some just aren't willing to risk it all to pursue their dreams.

## 2. Amount of time and effort required

Building a successful business takes a lot of time and effort. In fact, almost half of all entrepreneurs say they work more than 44 hours each week, and many even work 60 hours or more on a weekly basis. 93 percent of those surveyed in the Kauffman study said that the time and effort barrier was an important factor in deterring entrepreneurship.

All of these long hours of tough work can lead to sleep disorders, hypertension, weight gain, and relationship problems. Being an entrepreneur isn't for the weak or the lazy. It's hard work, but it can be done.

## 3. Difficulty in raising capital

Starting a business takes money. Just how much money it takes depends on the type of business you start, how well you utilize free and low-cost resources, and how organized you are. There are many different paths entrepreneurs can take to get the money they need, such as tapping personal savings, getting a loan from a bank, pitching a venture capital firm, borrowing from family and friends, or bringing in new business partners. Each path presents its own unique challenges.

According to the Kauffman study, 91 percent of business owners surveyed said that difficulty in raising capital was an important barrier to entrepreneurship.

## 4. Lack of business management skills

Transforming a great idea into a great business requires strong management competence. Just think of all the different moving parts that go into a functioning business. From sales to accounting to employee management, there's so much to manage and some simple oversight or mistake could bring your business to its knees.

Successful entrepreneurs know how to manage a business or they bring in someone to help guide them down the right path to managing their business effectively. However, 89 percent of business owners surveyed said that a lack of business management skills is one of the major barriers to entrepreneurial success.

## 5. Lack of knowledge of how to start a business

Eighty-four percent of company founders surveyed by Kauffman said that lack of knowledge about how to start a business was a key barrier to entrepreneurship. There's a lot that goes into launching a business, and the average person doesn't know everything it takes to get a business off the ground.

Having a great idea is a very small part of the battle. You have to know how to turn that idea into a real business, and that involves everything from filing the correct legal documents to creating a business plan to hiring employees. It can be overwhelming for someone who lacks prior experience in starting a business.

## 6. Unawareness of industry and markets

Knowing your industry, the latest trends, your competitors, your target audience, and market opportunities is important to building a successful business. Unfortunately, many entrepreneurs lack this critical knowledge. According to Kauffman research, 83 percent of company entrepreneurs surveyed said that unawareness about the industry and markets was a common barrier to entrepreneurial success.

What's the risk that comes with not knowing your industry and markets? You won't be able to identify good opportunities that you can capitalize on with your product and service offerings. You also won't have the familiarity with your competition that you need to have if you want to gain a competitive edge and increase your market share. Basically, your business will be like a ship without a rudder—no direction and little chance of getting where you want it to go.

### 7. Family or financial pressures to keep a traditional, steady job

Anybody who has ever walked away from a "real job" to become an entrepreneur has undoubtedly been subjected to ridicule from those who think it's foolish and irresponsible to not have a traditional, steady job. Seventy-three percent of those surveyed by Kauffman believed that family or financial pressures to keep a "real job" were significant issues contributing to entrepreneurial failure.

The truth is there will be people in your life who won't share your vision of becoming a successful entrepreneur. Instead, they will constantly plant seeds of doubt in your mind and pressure you to give up. Often times, this pressure comes from a sincere place of love and concern for your well-being, but you have to be strong enough to continue on the path that you know is right regardless of what others may say.

So there you have it, seven top barriers to entrepreneurial success. The bottom line is this—there is no easy path to success. If you want to be a successful entrepreneur, you're going to have to find a way to overcome imposing barriers.

### Overcoming the Barriers

During the 1800s, as the Atlantic gateway to the United States, New York was a wildly growing city bursting with greatness. Yet waterways as the Hudson and East Rivers limited the integration and thus the growth of the city's Five Boroughs. New York City needed a bridge if it was to ever reach its potential. An immigrant family from Germany by the name of Roebling had the vision, skill and persistence to build that bridge. John Roebling, a civil engineer, laid out original plans but died from injuries received in a ferry crash. His son, Washington Roebling, became chief engineer of the bridge construction after his father's death.

There were tremendous engineering challenges Washington faced to successfully build this bridge, some of them requiring new and innovative approaches for that time. Since it was to be a suspension bridge larger than anything done before, he used a design of steel cables instead of iron for the first time. The towers of the bridge were extremely tall and strong weighing 60,000 tons each, and had to be driven down below the riverbed into the bedrock below for a strong foundation. To accomplish this, he had innovative caissons developed with shafts, which were air- and water-tight chambers that enabled the workers to work below the water so to dig out the foundations and install the towers.

However there was at that time a mysterious sickness that afflicted the workers in the caissons. Today we know it as the bends or decompression sickness. Since Washington was a hands-on engineer in overseeing the work, he too spent significant time in the caissons. The "Caisson Sickness" had serious effects on his health leading to paralysis where he spent the rest of his life bound to a wheel chair as a paraplegic.

When this happened, then Emily his wife, who was only twenty-nine years old at the time, took the lead in overseeing the building of the bridge as his assistant. Amazingly, she took care of her husband, listened to his instructions, relayed these to the construction foremen and oversaw the construction. She was determined to see the bridge completed.

When the Brooklyn Bridge was officially opened on May 24$^{th}$, 1883, Emily Roebling was the first person to cross over, in front of dignitaries, including the President of the United States, and thousands of New Yorkers. Building the Brooklyn Bridge took fourteen years, 600 workers of whom 27 lost their lives, the leadership of a family where a father lost his life, a husband was crippled, and a wife who unfailingly took care of family and in the end led completion of the bridge. Their vision, skill, innovation, commitment and persistence built a bridge overcoming barriers that led to the future success and growth of a successful city.

### Building Bridges Over Barriers

Likewise, entrepreneurial success is about how well you build a bridge to get over barriers, so you can overcome the challenges of starting and building a business. I truly believe that the entrepreneur who successfully bridges over these barriers has a significant opportunity of realizing extraordinary benefits.

The good news is that you too can build strong, durable bridges to get past every major barrier to entrepreneurial success. This bridge building will take a lot of work, but with the right plan, hard work, persistence and a dash of good fortune, you can make your way to the other side where success awaits you.

That's why I wrote this book. During the following chapters of the book, we will explore each of these seven top barriers to entrepreneurial success. Each chapter will further define the barrier being discussed, identify its causes, present real world examples and case studies, and most importantly, provide potential solutions for building bridges across the barrier.

Of course, this is just a single book, and there simply isn't enough space in one book to exhaustively cover every data point of information or possible permutation of its main and minor subjects such as this one. Each barrier is complex enough that it could warrant its own book; so for now, I've made a good faith effort to make you more aware of the challenges and share with you thoughts that can be a genesis in your mind to your own bridge over challenges you may face.

Eventually, I will cover these and other important topics in even more detail throughout the rest of my "Successful Entrepreneur Advisor" series. I encourage you to frequently check www.successfulentrepreneuradvisor.com for updates regarding new books and products and other resources that will help you in your entrepreneurial journey.

No matter what stage of the entrepreneurial journey you currently find yourself in, you'll find this book helpful. It has something for everyone, including:

- **The person who wants to be an entrepreneur.** This person has seriously considered the idea of leaving the rat race and becoming an entrepreneur. They often already have great business ideas, but they just don't know how to bring them to fruition. Others want their own business but aren't sure how to leverage their experience and skills. Often times, this person keeps their entrepreneurial dreams a secret, perhaps because they're afraid friends and family may shoot them down, but this fear could be nothing in comparison to the regret they may experience by not taking the chance to realize their dreams.

- **The person who has tried to be an entrepreneur but without success**. Success doesn't always come easy, and many entrepreneurs have tried and failed. However, it's been found that serial entrepreneurs have a higher success rate than first-timers. In other words, if you've failed in the past, that doesn't mean you should give up your dream of owning a business. In fact, when you try again after a failed endeavor, you actually have a better chance of succeeding. Lots of these folks had gumption and heart but perhaps could have used more motivation and direction with a clear business strategy and roadmap to success.

- **The person who is an entrepreneur and has tasted success but wants more**. This person is ready to take it to the next level and knows that they can achieve even greater things. They're ready to try new ideas, approaches, and methods that can enable the progress necessary to grow their business and increase their wealth.

My desire is that you will find this book beneficial and balanced, which means you will have various emotional experiences as you read it. Some will realize they are not suited to starting a business, others will learn more about the challenges and rewards so they may forge ahead. I plan to give you the cold, hard truth, along with its difficulties, but I also will constantly motivate you and remind you there is help and there are solutions to overcome the barriers to starting or growing a business as an entrepreneur, so you can reap the rewards. At times, it may feel like a slap in the face, and other times a pat on the back. Sometimes like a taste of honey, others like a mouthful of vinegar; even sweet and sour in the same paragraph.

Yet in the end, I want you to feel like you're armed with more facts, better prepared for problems that may arise, and better equipped to take action; so you can build bridges for yourself and overcome the barriers that stand in your way on your journey to entrepreneurial success.

Let's cross some bridges!

# 4

## HOW TO OVERCOME BARRIER #1: LACK OF WILLINGNESS OR ABILITY TO TAKE RISKS

"Never was anything great achieved without danger."

~ Niccolo Machiavelli

What does Oprah Winfrey have in common with Evel Knievel? How is Donald Trump the same as Harry Houdini? What makes Steve Jobs and tight-rope walker Philippe Petit kindred spirits?

Give up? All of these people are risk takers. Some of them take risks like jumping a motorcycle over a canyon, getting buried alive in a straitjacket, or blindfolding themselves and letting a bull gore them. Others take risks that might not create as much of a visual spectacle, but are big risks just the same, such as walking away from a great job to launch a television network, putting tons of money on the line and overcoming bankruptcy multiple times to pursue new business ventures, or dropping out of college to eventually take the tech world by storm and launch a line of game-changing electronics.

Entrepreneurs are risk takers. We each take our own unique risks in order to pursue our dreams. Some of us risk our money; others risk our healthcare and overall happiness. Some of us take smart, calculated risks; others are reckless and take foolish risks that really had no chance of succeeding in the first place.

But, for every one of those entrepreneurs who has the courage to take a risk and follow their dream, there are thousands of others who had a dream . . . and that's it . . . they had a dream.

So, what enables one person to grab the "golden ring" and another to feel it's out of reach? What gives one person the willingness or courage it takes to jump into entrepreneurship and another to dip his toe in and quickly pull it back?

It all boils down to the unwillingness or inability to take risks, and at the root of this is fear...the fear of risk.

The 2009 research report by The Kauffman Foundation of Entrepreneurship, Anatomy of an Entrepreneur: Making of a Successful Entrepreneur, which surveyed 549 business founders in various industries, found that the 98 percent of those surveyed cited a "lack of willingness or ability to take risks" as their primary barrier to starting a business. And, of that 98 percent, half considered this barrier to be extremely challenging and important.

Ninety-eight percent! That's almost 100 percent! In other words, nearly every entrepreneur struggles with the lack of willingness or ability to take the leap of faith necessary to starting a business and pursuing a dream. Talk about tipping the scales.

## What Are We So Afraid Of?

In the article "Individual Psychotherapy: How It Can Help You Overcome Anxiety About Risk Taking", Patricia H. Hecht, MFT said, "To obtain important goals in life, individuals must take calculated risks. However, many people focus on failing to reach the goals they want, or they are afraid of the unknown consequences of failing. People are not sure of their own abilities, or afraid of not succeeding in the attempt. People often imagine irrational consequences of failing which frighten them."

Why are most people scared away from becoming entrepreneurs? As an entrepreneur, you assume the risk for your business. According to Lightbulb Press Dictionary of Financial Terms, "risk is the possibility you'll lose money or make less than you anticipate based on the performance of the investments you make." MacMillan Dictionary defines "risk" on a more personal level: "[Risk is] the possibility that something unpleasant or dangerous might happen."

However you choose to define risk, the fact remains the same: All entrepreneurs face some level of risk, and many would-be entrepreneurs are just too scared to take the risk required to start a business. That's because the harsh reality is that most business endeavors will fail, and for some, that's just too frightening a proposition to consider.

Consider these statistics:

- First-time entrepreneurs have an 18 percent chance of succeeding.

- Entrepreneurs who have succeeded in a prior venture have a 30 percent chance of succeeding in their next venture.

- First-time entrepreneurs have an 11.7 percent chance of success when funded by VC firms with little experience.

- Owners of small businesses annually file an estimated 260,000 to 315,000 bankruptcies.

I could fill this entire chapter with similar statistics, but I don't want to do that because that's not what this book is about. Yes, I want you to understand that there are certainly serious risks to becoming an entrepreneur, but I'm not trying to scare you off. In fact, I'm trying to do just the opposite. What's most important to know is there are things you can do to minimize risks and increase your chances of success.

Rational or normal fear of risk is a good thing. It protects you from danger and foolish actions. You, no doubt, use reason to take calculated risks on a regular basis. But when it comes to the "big" risks, like starting your own business, fear can often take control and leave you paralyzed. Without risk taking, people would not move forward in their personal and professional lives.

**Taking a Risk Isn't the Same as Being Reckless**

You hear stories and some are true, of someone starting a business and they are down to the their last dollar, have a second mortgage against their home which is past due, keep several credit cards that are maxed to their limits, and their personal life relationships are almost gone. I don't think it has to happen this way, but it does for some because of a lack of preparation for potential risks they could face.

But this isn't how all entrepreneurs live. Some of this is a stereotype, of course. Many people think of entrepreneurs being the reckless type, but as we've already established, studies have shown that risk prevents most from taking the entrepreneurial path and those that do, by and large, are not gamblers.

Yes, entrepreneurs are risk takers but so are all people. From driving to work to eating unhealthy food to crossing the street, nearly everything we do entails risk. We can't eliminate these risks; all we can do is know what they are and mitigate them to the best of our ability.

The same can be said for the savvy entrepreneur. Entrepreneurs do not think of risk in terms of eliminating it, but rather knowing what they are, so they can develop a sound plan for reducing risk and unwelcome surprises. Wise entrepreneurs only take smart business risks after carefully weighing the pros and cons and making a plan that provides the best chance of success. They understand the inherent ambiguity that comes with starting a new business, and they are willing to work hard to overcome any obstacles that may try to prevent them from realizing their vision.

Smart entrepreneurs are not scared away by thoughts of failure, but instead they think of it as a learning experience in their continuing quest for their goals. Just as people wear seatbelts, map their routes, and look both ways when driving through intersections to mitigate the risk of driving, the entrepreneur performs exhaustive research and careful planning to mitigate the risk of starting a business. Drivers accept that they could get blindsided at any moment, just as entrepreneurs accept that an unexpected surprise could pop up and do harm to their business.

That's not to imply that entrepreneurs aren't afraid of risk. Even the most seasoned, successful entrepreneur is afraid of losing money, not making enough money, getting in over his head, causing damage to personal relationships, and many other things. But rather than letting that fear create paralysis, they use it to make themselves plan more carefully, work harder, and manage better until they reach their goals.

Many entrepreneurs will credit their success in part to their preparedness. This preparation comes in many different forms, from prior work experience to market research to business strategy development. Smart entrepreneurs understand that the harder you work, the luckier you get. They understand that Mr. Preparation is always the most likely to meet Ms. Opportunity.

There are stupid risks and smart risks – make sure it's the latter. Applying research, creativity, strategy, planning, and perseverance makes it the latter.

Successful entrepreneurs are not those who take foolish, unnecessary risks; they're part risk taker, part visionary. They enjoy the challenge of a new venture. They're able to analyze and calculate risks without letting fear enter the equation. They are able to see the potential of a new venture, and they have the drive and perseverance to make it happen.

**Potential Risk Factors Involved with Entrepreneurship**

There are many types of risks that entrepreneurs can face. Some may have a minimal impact and can be managed easily; others may threaten the viability and success of the business. While reading through the rest of this chapter, I encourage you to consider these risks and to truly think about your comfort level with taking risks. Knowing how much risk you can comfortably tolerate will help you determine if a certain venture is one you should attempt.

Please understand that this chapter doesn't represent an effort to identify any and every potential risk an entrepreneur may face. It is variable depending on many factors and cannot be possibly known without a risk assessment of the specific entrepreneur and their venture. However, you will learn about some of the common risk factors involved with entrepreneurship, and more importantly, you will begin to understand an attitude and approach that will help you build bridges over risks you may face as an entrepreneur.

While there are a number of risks involved with entrepreneurship, and the risks will vary depending on the background and abilities of each person, they each fall into one of two major categories: intrinsic barriers and extrinsic barriers.

## Intrinsic Barriers

Intrinsic barriers are those that originate from within...those things contained within you. This is fear and doubt in your own body, mind, and abilities. PsychologyCampus.com defines intrinsic motivation as, "striving inwardly to be competent at something and to reward yourself inwardly."

Below are some of the intrinsic barriers you may face.

### Fear of Failure

Nearly every budding entrepreneur starting a new business struggles with the fear of failure. When contemplating becoming an entrepreneur, all the "what ifs" come into play and reinforce the other fear factors related to entrepreneurship. You start thinking about the overwhelming percentage of business ventures that fail, and you worry that your business will suffer the same fate. You also think about all the small businesses that have to file for bankruptcy, and you tremble in your boots imagining this to be your future. All of this is good food for thought. You don't want to jump blindly into a risky situation, but you have to be careful that this healthy food for thought doesn't also feed your fear and turn it into a monster.

Interestingly, there doesn't seem to be much rhyme or reason as to who faces the most pressure from fear of failure. In other words, all types of people are afraid of failure, but we allow that fear to affect us to different degrees. Some use that fear to fuel a stronger work ethic; others let it overcome them and prevent them from chasing their dreams.

Doing your homework, such as reading this book, should help alleviate your fear of failure. Knowing what to expect is a key element to overcoming fear. After you know what to expect, you just have to be as prepared as possible for the "what ifs" and be persistent.

It's well known that before someone reaches success, the path getting there is usually riddled with passing defeats and possible failures. Take Henry Ford as an example. He faced several failed automotive endeavors, including the Detroit Automobile Co., before achieving success with the release of the Model T.

Or what about Frederick W. Smith, founder of FedEx? After revolutionizing the mail delivery industry in the 1970s, Smith started an electronic delivery service called Zapmail in 1984. The service was supposed to compete with fax machines, but it was a miserable failure, costing the company about $350 million in just two years. But Smith and FedEx recovered and are still a smashing success to this day.

The point is that it won't always be smooth sailing, but with a sound business strategy and relentless drive, you can be successful. Keep this in mind, so the speed bumps along the way won't be a killer surprise.

Napoleon Hill, in his book *Think & Grow Rich* (1960), said that "more than five hundred of the most successful men this country has ever known told the author their greatest success came just one step beyond the point at which defeat had overtaken them" (p. 23).

## Fear of Success and Responsibilities

On the complete opposite end of the spectrum from fear of failure there lies the fear of success. While some may laugh at the thought of this, it's a real barrier to risk taking. Its affect can stop a wannabe entrepreneur from getting out of the gate.

On a conscious level we're all pretty much geared toward success, whether it is focused on our careers, schoolwork, or in our personal life. But, for most of us, our environment, upbringing, or experiences has a sneaky hold on us. We've been trained to believe we're not worthy of success, or that success will change our lives in an uncomfortable way, or that the more successful you become, the greater the eventual fall.

In the article "Fear of Success: How to Overcome It," Bill Cole, an authority on peak performance, explains that there are several reasons why someone may fear success. To paraphrase, these reasons include:

- Change is frightening

- You will be expected to succeed

- Your performance level will need to increase

- Success is an attention getter

- It may take a toll on your family or private life

- You question your ability to make it happen

To further shed light on the subject, Lisa Fritscher in her article "Fears of Failure and Success" explains, "Research has shown that both conditions [fear of failure and fear of success] share many of the same symptoms. Both are marked by anxiety symptoms in certain situations [and] both conditions can be crippling, leading the sufferer to take few risks and make only safe, conservative choices."

She adds that fear of success can also be related to "the level of control that the sufferer feels in his or her own life." Individuals who perceive extrinsic (outside) factors as being in control seem to have a higher tendency to fall prey to fear of success. "It could be that they do not feel that their success has been earned, or it could be that they fear outside forces may take away their success."

Along with success comes increased responsibility, thus the fear of responsibility factor. Although you may be able to delegate some of your responsibility as you become more and more successful, on the journey there the ball is entirely in your hands. You will be where the buck begins and stops.

Larry David, co-creator of *Seinfeld* (one of the most successful sitcoms of all time), has often said that when the show was doing its initial pilot run of five episodes, he prayed the network wouldn't pick it up. Why? Because he didn't want the responsibility of having to manage the workload of writing an entire season's worth of material. In other words, he was afraid to succeed. Of course, *Seinfeld* did get picked up, and it made David a very wealthy man. The comedian who once searched for places to stay if he became homeless built up an estimated net worth of more than $500 million, according to some reports.

It's only human to be a bit concerned or anxious over this success factor. Not everyone wants the huge responsibility that comes with running a business, requiring you to do things like finding all the resources to run and grow your business, making all the decisions, being in control from soup-to-nuts, from creation to marketing to sales, networking, finding qualified talent, knowing the legal and accounting aspects of running a business…the list goes on.

This is where preparation comes into play. Before you get too far into the process of starting your own business, spend time researching what is involved and do an honest self-analysis to determine if you can handle it and, more importantly, if you want to handle it. If you find yourself lacking, ask for help. You may have to seek the advice of professionals to get on the right track, but it could be well worth the investment. Don't let pride or fear stop you from looking for information and help to fill in the gaps you think you may have.

## Doubting Your Abilities

At some point in your life, I bet you've dealt with self-doubt. Maybe you've wondered if you're good looking enough, smart enough, experienced enough, talented enough, young enough, strong enough...is any of this ringing a bell yet? Most people usually don't realize their own potential. They're uncertain as to whether they have the ability needed to not only start a business, but to get it off the ground and really make it succeed.

Audra Quinn, in an article for Pepperdine Magazine, titled "Diagram of an Entrepreneur," wrote, "Bill Gates. Mary Kay. Richard Branson. Thomas Edison. Debbi Fields. None of these successful entrepreneurs ever graduated from college, nor did they pursue formal education in business or entrepreneurship. Yet from Microsoft to Virgin to Mrs. Fields, they redefined what it takes to turn good ideas into lucrative businesses."

Patricia H. Hecht explains, "People may have the abilities and talents to do many things in life and achieve spectacular goals, but only the rare person does not have to struggle and risk to achieve his or her goals."

Our limitations are usually self-imposed. Napoleon Hill said, "We foolishly believe that our own limitations are the proper measure of limitations."

So, even for those who are aware of their abilities, there will be some elements of fear of the unknown and even a bit of self-doubt with any new venture, whether personal or professional. It's a matter of facing these fears and doubts head on, overcoming them, and moving forward.

Consider these four strategies to conquer self-doubt:

**1. Knowledge is power:** Research everything that's involved in starting your own business. For example, in a later chapter of this book, we'll learn about the approach to gaining more knowledge of industries and markets. Doing this will help alleviate some of the fear of the unknown and possibly give you the confidence you need to move forward.

**2. Determine if your fears are warranted:** Often, we're our own worst enemy. It's possible you're overly critical of yourself, or you're overestimating what actually needs to be done, or you're amplifying what skills you'll need. Evaluate the situation before jumping to conclusions and blowing things out of proportion.

**3. Take action:** If you lack the knowledge or skills needed to become an entrepreneur, take action and get the skills or tools you'll need for success. This action can be in the form of education, hiring a mentor and coach, gathering online information, or taking part in an entrepreneurial apprenticeship. Don't be complacent; work toward your goals.

**4. Create a business strategy:** This is essential when contemplating any type of business. It's the only way you'll be able to determine what will be needed and how much it will cost. As with any planning, make your plans realistic and your goals achievable. Hiring a professional business advisor to help with developing your business strategy is a great way to ensure you head down the right path to success.

Learn more at www.successfulentrepreneuradvisor.com about how a business advisor can assist you with successful strategies like these for the success of your entrepreneurial efforts.

## Many Other Intrinsic Barriers

As already mentioned, this chapter isn't going to list every possible risk barrier that's out there. That's not my goal. My goal is to help you develop a mindset that will prime you to build a bridge over any barrier that may arise, whether expected or unexpected.

However, I will briefly touch on a particular few other intrinsic barriers entrepreneurs may struggle with:

- **Lack of people skills**—Many entrepreneurs lack the people skills necessary to develop networks, alliances, find the right employees, make sales, and grow their business in a multitude of other ways. Not all of us are outgoing and comfortable around strangers, but you need to develop confidence in yourself so you can meet the right people to help your business succeed.

- **Uncertainty of how one's self will handle adversity**— Many would-be entrepreneurs are simply scared about how they will react when trouble arises. They lack confidence in their ability to adapt to any situation and build bridges over new barriers. Know thyself, be confident in your abilities, and take strategic action to prepare for skillfully conquering any barrier placed in your way.

- **Waiting for perfection**—I've known many wannabe entrepreneurs who are always waiting for the perfect time to do this or that. They're waiting until they get their service or product perfect before starting. They're waiting for the perfect opportunity to present itself in the marketplace. And they keep waiting…and waiting…and waiting. Perfection is the enemy of the good. Start with small measured successes and then build to the major ones.

## Extrinsic Barriers

While intrinsic barriers originate inside the entrepreneur, extrinsic barriers are those that come from outside of the entrepreneur. Encyclopedia.com defines extrinsic motivations as, "an incentive to do something that arises from factors outside the individual, such as rewards or punishments."

Since these extrinsic barriers in addition to one's own psyche are at work, you will need to filter them out to get a clear view of what's holding you back from becoming the entrepreneur you want to be and the entrepreneur you should be. Below is a list of some common extrinsic barriers that can cultivate an unwillingness or inability to take risks.

## Personal Finances

The wannabe entrepreneur or the small business owner struggling to stay afloat both fight an unseen enemy – the fear of poverty. Hill said that fear of poverty is "the most destructive fear" (p. 224). The reason for its position at the top of the basic fears list is because "it is the most difficult to master" (p. 225).

This fear comes in many different forms, including:

- **The loss of an income**—While fear of poverty is at the top of the basic fears list, loss of income is at the top of the fear-of-poverty list. The wannabe entrepreneur has a lot to give up if he or she decides to take the leap. The fear of losing a steady paycheck that puts food on your table, a roof over your head, and clothes on your back, has stopped many a wannabe entrepreneur. For many they forego any salary in the early phases of their business, so there must have been the previous accrual of sufficient savings or successful raising of capital from other sources that will tide them over until the business is generating enough cash flow to make a living. For this reason, many entrepreneurs wisely start their new business enterprise while continuing to work their current job, and in many cases, these entrepreneurs start a business that is a natural extension of their work experience. In other words, they are doing what they know, thus increasing their chance of success.

- **The loss of health insurance**—Usually included in that steady paycheck is a health insurance benefit. It's understood that the young, healthy, and single individual may not deem this a significant consideration, but the majority of people do. Medical care for pregnancy and children can be very expensive, and then there are the unexpected expenses of prescription drugs, hospital stays, surgical costs, and a host of other medical expenses that can really pile up at the most inopportune time. The loss of health insurance is certainly a significant fear.

- **Retirement plan**—Most employers offer their workers some form of retirement plan. This is something prospective entrepreneurs will need to consider when contemplating chasing their dreams. The questions swirl around your head. What will happen to your treasured nest egg? Will you be able to continue saving for old age? Will you need to dip into your retirement savings or worse yet, will you have to empty it out just to stay afloat? Will Social Security still be available? If so, will it be enough? The questions go on and on. About one-third of small-business owners do not have a personal or business-sponsored retirement plan such as a

401(k), a SEP IRA, or deferred annuity, according to a new survey from the non-profit the American College. "The lack of retirement planning by so many people is stunning, especially since business owners have no one else to rely on when it comes to putting their retirement plans in place," said Mary Quist-Newins, Director of the State Farm Center for Women and Financial Services at The American College.

- **Other benefits**—Along with health insurance, steady employment usually affords the worker additional perks, such as vacation time, sick days, possibly a flexible work schedule, and opportunities to earn additional rewards or perks for achieving company objectives. Will you be able to live or be content without these perks?

- **Raising capital**—Do you have the financial ability to start a new business on your own? Starting a business costs money, and if you don't have enough money, you'll need to find investors, financing, or possibly a business partner or two. Reid Hoffman, former executive vice president at PayPal and cofounder of LinkedIn, compares the capital raising aspect of entrepreneurship to a plane taking off on a runway. The more money (backing) you require/acquire, the longer your runway, but the hurdle at the end of the runway is so much greater, as is the possible fall.

We will discuss this in more detail in a following chapter.

## Family

We all like to be supported in our pursuit of our dreams. Whether it comes in the form of an encouraging word, a pat on the back for a job well done, or just the knowledge that someone believed in you and wants you to succeed, it's always nice to feel supported. And in most cases, we turn to our families to get this support.

Unfortunately, not all families are supportive. You very well might have people in your family who think you're crazy for wanting to take the leap to become an entrepreneur. If your family discourages you and lists the many reasons why you shouldn't start a small business, or they simply don't have faith in you, you will have a constant struggle on your hands. Whether their reasons are valid—such as not being able to sustain the lifestyle they're use to, not being able to provide the fundamental needs of your family (which includes food and shelter), not having you around as much because of the time drain of starting a new business, or losing the precious nest egg—their concerns are obviously yours. In other words, you can't just ignore them.

Likewise, whatever struggles you face as an entrepreneur, your family faces them as well. They need to be on your team. They need to be prepared. Spousal forbearance, family support, and work-life balance were among the most commonly cited challenges faced by entrepreneurs. If the business makes it and does well but costs you your marriage or your relationship with your kids, were you really a success?

This is personal, but I was lucky in the spousal forbearance and support category. I hit the jackpot. My loving wife's support has helped me succeed in more ways than I could ever explain or quantify. It has been very important to me in business, and it's a subject I'll touch on in further detail later in this book.

## Other Extrinsic Barriers

Again, I can't list every potential extrinsic barrier, but I hope you're starting to understand the barriers and are developing the mindset and skill set that are required for overcoming challenges that may present itself to you on your journey to entrepreneurial success.

However, there are a couple other extrinsic barriers I'd like to touch on briefly before we move forward.

- **Market risk**—Is there really a market for your product or service? Can you make money? Do you know your competition? Have you done the research and analysis necessary for creating a strategy that leads to success? Or are you just making assumptions? You know what happens when you assume, so make sure you really take the time to assess market risk before moving forward with your venture.

- **Lack of realistic expectations**—You have a great idea, and you're just sure that you're going to be making money hand over fist in no time at all. But the truth is that it's probably going to take a lot of time, hard work, capital, and luck before you start to see the results you hoped for. Too many entrepreneurs have unrealistic expectations, and they aren't prepared for the battle that lies ahead. Get your expectations in check. It might help to have a professional advisor with an unbiased perspective take another look at your business idea and strategy to ensure its feasibility.

## How to Prepare for and Manage Risk

You can't eliminate all risks. All you can do is manage and minimize them.

Oftentimes, business owners rely on their experience and intuition to manage risk, but not all new entrepreneurs have enough experience to deal with the surprise situations that come with starting and operating a business. And the more unique or complex the business venture, the more potential there is for unknown or unexpected risks to arise. You must be prepared!

In this chapter, we are looking at a number of common risks faced by entrepreneurs, but I don't list them all—that would be impossible. And that's the point. I can't know every possible risk that's out there for you, but you can develop a mentality and basic strategy for overcoming any unwelcome surprises that might try to trip you up.

## R.M.A.P

Risk management is the way in which potentially adverse effects from risks are mitigated. To begin your personal management of risk, think of these letters: R.M.A.P. They are important to minimizing your risk and enhancing your potential opportunities.

The first use of these letters is in thinking about your Risk MAP. It's just like using a GPS Mapping system, which I use in marine travel with my boat. When boating, this electronic navigation system shows me where I am, the pathway to my destination, the channels I must stay in, and the hazards I am to avoid, so that I don't damage or ground the vessel and will reach my destination safely.

For your vessel—your business—it's the same. Taking the approach of creating your own business Risk MAP will show you ahead of time where the hazards are so you can avoid them and successfully reach your goals. Proceeding without this guidance is a sure-fire way to create a business that lacks direction and growth.

To develop your Risk MAP, just follow these steps:

1. Identify the real risks that are involved.

2. Assess the probabilities of the risks occurring.

3. Evaluate the consequences of those risks if they occur.

4. Prioritize the risks according to their significance by classifying them according to whether they are of major or minor consequence and their likelihood.

To the uninitiated some of this may seem a bit technical, and for best results, it is good to have an experienced advisor to assist. An experienced advisor will have various methods and tools to assist with developing your Risk MAP, such as frameworks with templates, analysis methods like SWOT, and modeling techniques. Upon completing correctly, you would have mapped out your business risks, creating a clear picture of what is important to focus on.

The next use of R.M.A.P. is for the Risk Management Action Plan. Once you have mapped out and prioritized the risks that have the highest chance of occurring and the most significant consequences, you need to identify what you can do to mitigate those risks in a cost-effective manner. Adding actions to the risk evaluation matrix is developing your action plan. You will assign an action for each risk according to its ranking.

From the risk map, you will see some risks are not a big deal (low likelihood and minor consequence), which you can ignore, avoid, or reduce their likelihood of occurring. For example, you might run the risk of getting a flat tire on the company van, but assuming you keep decent tires on your car and take care of them, that's a small risk with a minor consequence. Some risks you can ignore until a time in the future; for example, risk to business equipment can be ignored until it's time for the next scheduled maintenance, assuming regular maintenance is done. Others may have some immediate impact but can be managed appropriately (slightly higher likelihood and consequence), like your lead salesperson gets the flu and is out a week, but you have trained a backup who can pick up the slack for a short time.

Other risks may threaten the viability and success of the business (high likelihood and of major consequence). These are company killers. They are the key risks for which you must have an action plan in place to protect you and your business. Perhaps your business is on the coast where you could have a hurricane or an earthquake, so you must obtain adequate insurance and have a business continuity plan in the event of a disaster. Maybe you have a key person in the business or a key customer whose loss would be catastrophic. What if there is a loss of this resource to the business? What is your plan to mitigate this? Are you training a backup? Are you actively increasing your customer base so you're not relying so heavily on one client to keep the lights on? Are you actively monitoring the situation?

Things can and will happen. And you'll get plenty of practice at responding to situations throughout your entrepreneurial journey as unanticipated events and emergencies are certain to arise. You don't have a crystal ball to where you can anticipate everything, but if you take the time to develop an approach mindset, and strategy for responding to risks, you can minimize the damage of these unwelcome surprises.

Now, you might be reading through this and think it's going to take some time and effort for you to effectively manage risks, but remember you're dealing with the severest barrier facing entrepreneurs. Ninety-eight percent of entrepreneurs struggle with managing risk. It's an essential task that's absolutely vital to protecting your business, and with the right method and templates it doesn't require that much time and effort.

In the end, this effort can save you money and heartache, and it can help prevent failure. Don't let risk paralyze you. Be pragmatic, be informed, be prepared, and be proactive. If you need help with it, get in touch with us.

"All courses of action are risky, so prudence is not in avoiding danger (it's impossible), but calculating risk and acting decisively. Make mistakes of ambition and not mistakes of sloth. Develop the strength to do bold things, not the strength to suffer."

~ Niccolo Machiavelli

# 5

## HOW TO OVERCOME BARRIER #2:
## AMOUNT OF TIME AND EFFORT REQUIRED

"Time is more valuable than money. You can get more money, but you cannot get more time."

~ Jim Rohn

There's an old quote from Napoleon Hill I like that goes like this: "Great achievement is usually born of great sacrifice, and is never the result of selfishness." I ask you to keep this quote in mind as you read this chapter. Make no mistake. If you want to be a successful entrepreneur, you're going to have to make sacrifices. Lots of them. You're going to have to sacrifice your time and energy to achieve your goals, and if anybody tells you otherwise, they're lying to you.

That's why it didn't surprise me when I read that 93% of entrepreneurs surveyed said that the amount of time and effort required to be successful was an important barrier.

When you start your own business, you're not going to be working a nice, comfy 40-hour work week. But hey, that's one of the reasons you got into this, right? You wanted to kiss the 9-5 grind goodbye. What you may not have realized is that, by doing that, you now find yourself kissing the 9-9 grind hello. But that's OK isn't it? – because what you're doing your passionate about, or at least you better be. Passion for your entrepreneurial endeavor is what will provide the fuel necessary for exerting the time and effort required to gain success.

The good news? There are plenty of tactics you can use to overcome this major challenge. I'm not saying it will always be easy, but when you use the bridge-building approaches I provide later in this chapter, you'll be able to get more done in less time, all the while providing a way for your personal life away from work to still remain healthy and rewarding. So, when you read about the heavy demands placed on the entrepreneur's time and energy, don't get down. Follow your passion and also utilize bridge-building approaches, and you can overcome this barrier and reap the rewards that come with being a successful entrepreneur!

**Survey Says...**

A recent Gallup poll found that 26% of self-employed workers (entrepreneurs) say they work at least 60 hours per week. Furthermore, 49% of self-employed workers work more than 44 hours each week.

Still haven't broken a sweat yet? Don't worry, there's more. According to estimates from the U.S. Small Business Administration, the amount of uncompensated time entrepreneurs devote to starting new businesses is massive—7.7 billion hours in 1999 and 9.9 billion hours in 2005. Remember, these are the hours spent doing unpaid work.

The U.S. Small Business Administration has also extensively studied the amount of time it takes for entrepreneurs to actually get their businesses started, and here is what they found as detailed in The Small Business Economy:

"Only one-third of entrepreneurs will actually have a working business within the first six years. Over the same period, another one-third of these nascent entrepreneurs will disengage. Yet another one-third of these entrepreneurs will not have gotten past the earliest stages of the firm creation process in six years."

But surely putting in these long hours day in and day out helps you get a good night's sleep, right? Think again. Many entrepreneurs report sleeping just 4-6 hours per night. A study by Marianna Virtanen of the Finnish Institute of Occupational Health linked long days to sleep problems and disorders. A similar study of women entrepreneurs by The American College found that many business owners have poor sleeping habits, with a large percentage struggling to get sound sleep at night.

In 2006, the University of California, Irvine released a study finding that chronic workweeks of more than 51 hours can triple the risk of hypertension. And remember, more than one in four entrepreneurs works at least 60 hours per week. Add the fact that when you're working long hours and are constantly running on fumes, you likely aren't exercising or eating properly, and it's starting to become pretty clear why time and effort are such huge barriers to entrepreneurial success.

Now, I'm not saying all of this to scare you. Really, I'm not. But I am trying to give you a reality check. If you want any chance at building a successful business, you need to prepare yourself mentally and physically for the time and effort it's going to take. Nothing worth having comes easy, but if you're truly committed to putting in the work, you can achieve your biggest goals. The amount of success you have is in your hands, and by the time you finish this chapter, you'll know some proven strategies for overcoming the time and effort barrier to becoming a successful entrepreneur.

## What Do I Know about Hard Work?

I know what you're thinking: "It's easy for you to tell me I have to work long hours and go without sleep to be a successful entrepreneur. What do you know about hard work?" That's a fair question, and in this chapter I will share a just a bit of my experiences with you.

Allow me to refer back to when I was growing up as a poor country boy on a farm, where I quickly learned the value of hard work. My mother, especially, taught me that I could achieve anything I wanted to if I was willing to put in the work. I learned to work hard after school and on weekends so I could buy my clothes and items I wanted like a car. This served as a solid foundation that helped me reach my goals growing up and continues to help me to this day.

In college, I went to school during the day, worked in the evening to pay for it, and studied late at night. I might get a couple of hours of sleep on weekdays, but I set aside my weekends for sleeping. On top of all this, I got married and had a kid. Boy, do I have a knack for making things really tough on myself! Time and again, I hardly got any sleep and was completely exhausted, but still pushing forward because I had a goal in mind. I wanted to graduate and get out in the world and build a better life for myself and others. I refused to let anything stand in the way.

When I graduated, that wasn't the end of the hard work and long hours. Little did I know that everything thus far was just preparation for what was to come. When I was going through that business system engineering program boot camp, I mention it in the about the author section titled Journey of One Entrepreneur, where they try to make you or break you, it was during the winter. I remember being in a corner of the room by myself at 2 am and I could hear the howling of a strong winter wind around the outside corner of the building, while I was pushing to make a seemingly impossible deadline for a business system design and code. It was a lonely feeling, but I learned to keep my head down and keep working no matter what and you will get there.

There was the time working with the executives of a company where I had completed the assessment and had all the information but had to complete the go-forward strategy to present to the executive team first of the coming week. I went into that weekend not knowing the answers but after working all the way through had a path forward to consider for that meeting.

None of us as average entrepreneurs have unlimited money to support the businesses we start, so many times I have worked nights and weekends against deadlines to get parts of my businesses completed and up and running such as websites, marketing, product development, resource administration and more. There was also a time where I traveled and worked for days without sleep which I will mention more about in a bit. There have been many of these times of long hours. The point? None of this makes me special. It's just the challenges that anyone in entrepreneurial endeavors will have from time to time around time and effort.

## Why Does Being an Entrepreneur Require so Much Work?

You might be wondering just why entrepreneurs have to work so hard. Surely, there are ways around putting in 60+ hour work weeks, week in and week out, right? I'll get to the approaches for overcoming this barrier in a moment (and rest assured, there are many), but first, let me share some of the reasons that being an entrepreneur demands so much time and effort:

- **Entrepreneurs wear a lot of hats**—If you had visions of being the CEO who kicks his feet up on the desk and collects money while everyone else does all the hard work, you're not going to be a successful entrepreneur. More likely, you'll be handling all sorts of different tasks when you're first launching your business. You'll be writing a business plan, setting up your office/retail space, marketing your business, hiring and managing employees, managing projects, handling your accounting, interacting with customers...the list goes on and on. With your hands on every aspect of your business from top to bottom, you can already see how the typical entrepreneur's plate is overflowing. And we're just getting started!

- **The early stages of launching a business require the most work**—Earlier, we examined how years might be needed for an entrepreneur to get a business going. The early stages require the most work. Think about it like building a house. The construction phase takes a lot of work, doesn't it? You have to lay the foundation, frame the house, put in the electrical and plumbing, build the floors and walls, and put in all of the finishing touches that make it a beautiful house. Once the house is built, it doesn't require nearly as much work to maintain it. The same concept applies to building a business. Early on, there's a lot of work to be done. You have to get a sound business plan, study the competitive landscape, raise capital, get permits, build your physical business space, promote your business, hire employees...shall I go on?

- **Disorganization and irrelevant tasks create time clutter**—If you're managing every aspect of your business on your own, you're going to overlook things here and there. It's inevitable, and the harsh reality is that the average entrepreneur can be horribly disorganized. They overlook important tasks and things slip through the cracks, and later on, this increases their work load and creates time clutter. Then, there are the irrelevant tasks that create even more time clutter. How much time do you spend each day goofing around on Facebook, checking emails, or mindlessly surfing the web when you should be working? This makes your work days longer than they need to be.

- **Lack of knowledge slows you down**—In *Methodology of Business Studies*, lack of business knowledge is cited as one of the top barriers to successful entrepreneurship. *Entrepreneurship in Action* also focuses on this barrier, stating that most startup businesses fail within a few years because of a lack of business knowledge. Remember earlier when I listed all the different hats entrepreneurs have to wear? Unless you're a genius, you probably aren't knowledgeable in all the different aspects of running a business, so your lack of knowledge is going to slow you down and could lead to costly mistakes.

- **The competition never sleeps**—No matter what industry you're in, you have competitors, and those competitors have a head start on you because they've been around longer. You can't afford to take your foot off the pedal for even a split second, because as soon as you do, your competitors will drive off in the distance and you'll have to work even harder if you want to catch them.

- **When fires get started, you have to put them out**—When something goes wrong regarding your startup business, you're the one who will have to handle it. Burst pipe at your store? You have to drive there to minimize the damage and meet the plumber. Angry customer? You're the one who is going to have to speak with them and hopefully calm them down. An employee stole money out of the cash register? You're the one who will have to press charges and fire the employee. Any time fires get started (and believe me, fires will get started), you're the one who will have to put them out, so you're always on call.

- **There's always something to be done**—The bottom line is that there is always something to be done for your business. There will always be an email you can respond to, a marketing opportunity you need to take advantage of, payroll that needs to be processed, or a customer who needs attention. You could work 24/7, and there would still be more to be done.

## Building a Bridge Over the Time and Effort Barrier

An entrepreneur by the name of Henry Ford said, "It has been my observation that most people get ahead during the time that others waste." He would know. He is the person usually remembered as founder of the Ford Motor Company and the associated innovation of conveyor-based assembly lines with standard interchangeable parts for automobiles.

However, when you peer more deeply into his entrepreneurial life and earlier years leading up to Ford Motor, one finds that this was a guy that "never let the grass grow under his feet." He had always been one that put in the necessary time and effort to fulfill his goals.

He was raised on a farm but disliked it and had a passion for machinery. He became a self-taught mechanic and machinist as he worked on the farm machinery. He left the farm life and in Detroit gained a position as an apprentice in a machine shop where he worked 12 hours a day, six days a week. Later, he took a job working on steam engines during the day and repairing watches and clocks at night so he could pay all his living expenses. In addition, while working long hours he also attended business college to learn the skills he believed one day he would need for his own successful business.

Ultimately, it was while working a fulltime job and in his spare time and own funds he built his first "horseless carriage." Encouraged and with the backing of a wealthy Detroit business man, he went out on his own founding the Detroit Automobile Company. It was not successful but a great learning experience that in time led him along with a group of investors in establishing the Ford Motor Company. They introduced the first Model T automobile in 1908 that was innovatively produced so that it was affordable and easy to repair. This led to a proliferation of the auto and creation of the American Car Culture which Ford Motor Company is still an important part.

As I look at Henry Ford's success, I see one adept at overcoming the barrier of time and effort and passionate as an entrepreneur. Here was his own observation, "I do not believe a man can ever leave his business. He ought to think of it by day and dream of it by night."

Like my mom always told me, you can do anything you decide to do. If you're really serious and passionate about becoming a successful entrepreneur, you'll find ways to overcome the time and effort it demands. To help you do this, I'm going to share some of the tactics I've used over the years for getting the job done right, despite the time and energy it requires.

## Suck it up

Let me get the tough love out of the way first. Sometimes, I hear entrepreneurs complaining about how hard it is to run a business, but you know what? It *is* hard. If you didn't know that going into it, it probably didn't take you very long to figure it out. You chose this path, and the truth is that success isn't going to be handed to you. But you can be successful if you're willing to put in the hard work.

I know that it seems like there's not enough time for you to get everything done. Sometimes, we have to work long hours and only get a few hours of sleep each night until we get the job done. And I know it's true because I've stayed up for three days straight before because I wanted to get the job done.

As a principal of a consulting firm, I led a business program for a wealthy European family client that owned several businesses. They were looking to improve one of their businesses and implement new technology and processes.

The plan was to do part of the work at their facilities on the East Coast of the United States before later going to Europe to their facilities and headquarters to wrap it up. As the project was going along, however, I realized that the plan in place for implementing their new business model just wasn't right. There were aspects of its premise that were incorrect, and I had to tell them.

When I told the executives by email and phone about my findings, they immediately put me on a plane that day to fly out to their headquarters. So, I started my morning in the United States, was on a plane at noon, flew to Pittsburgh then to New York and on to Europe. I arrived at 7am local time on no sleep since working on the plane. I got to the hotel, changed, and went to offices to meet with my partners. After discussions and working on the presentation for the customer all day and night, I went back to my hotel, showered, and went to the airport to make a short flight to their headquarters. Still, I hadn't slept, but I should mention that I was fueled by this very strong, Italian coffee. Goodness, was I wired!

I arrived at their headquarters where I met with the executive board. I gave them the full presentation, and we spent the entire day and evening working out a new approach for the program. After finishing up in the evening, I caught my flight.

When I got in my room late that night, I looked at the time, and then realized I had gone three days without sleep! I was literally sick from a lack of sleep. It took me several days of rest to get back to normal.

My point? When you have to get things done, you can find a way. You may have to make some sacrifices, but if you're willing to put in the hard work, it can pay off. It can be done. It's just a matter of how badly you want it.

### *"It's not a sprint – it's a marathon"*

*"It's not a sprint – it's a marathon."* I heard this a lot from experienced partners when I first went into business consulting. I realized it was true as I experienced what the commitment to clients and success demanded. I'm not telling you this because I want to brag about how great I am. I'm not great. I'm no better than anyone else. And that's my point. We all have the potential to stay up late and work our tails off when we have to. You have the ability to do it. You just have to want to do it because your passionate about whatever it is. You have to be willing to fight yourself when your mind is telling you that it's too much work and that you need to go to sleep. Fighting against the resistance that lives inside of you is the toughest battle you'll ever have to fight.

I remember when I decided to run a marathon. I had run enough already in my life, both personally and competitively in school, to know that I would have to properly condition myself first if I was going to finish the marathon. So I joined a training program for fitness that was specially designed to train people for the marathon.

In this program, they taught us how to run, how to choose the correct running shoes and clothes to wear, and how to stay hydrated. They also gave us a running practice schedule to follow and led us on increasingly longer weekend training practice runs. The program had significant milestone runs to complete–12, 18, and 21 mile runs–prior to the 26.2 mile marathon. The first year I was in it I made it up to the 12-mile run. Then I suffered an Iliotibial band syndrome knee injury. I actually ran the 12-mile run with the injury, which was excruciating and dumb, but I was so committed and dedicated to achieving the marathon that I refused to quit. But after finishing that 12-mile run, I was sidelined for a while as I recovered from the injury.

During my recovery as I analyzed what happened and how, I ultimately realized the cause of my injury was poor running form and lack of stretching. So I adjusted my running style and always stretched before running. The next year I successfully completed the training program and found myself at the starting line of that marathon.

That year's marathon was a doozy (just my luck). Locally, we refer to it as the year of the Ice Marathon. Early that morning before the race, a storm came through with hard rain and the temperature plummeting down to freezing. As the starting gun sounded, the bridges on the streets–and there are many of them thanks to the plenitude of bayous and creeks in the city–were starting to freeze over. I remember seeing several runners slip and scratch themselves up badly due to the ice as they crossed the first bridge. I just kept to my pace and stayed extra careful.

Oddly enough, the cold would be a benefit to me, helping me complete the race. Around mile 16, I was running along and felt a strange sensation in my left foot, but I was able to keep going. Come to find out, I had turned my ankle and severely strained it, but because it was so cold and numb, I didn't realize it until later on after the race. The next day it was black and blue and really swollen.

But even the frigid weather could not help me at miles 22 through 26 as the exhaustion worked on my mind and screamed at me to quit. But quit I could not–I would not. My mind was made up to finish no matter what, and my body had already been conditioned so it could. I had prepared myself.

There are many lessons for the entrepreneur in this story. Successfully starting a business is much like marathon training and running. Some do not adequately prepare themselves. I believe many people quit just before the finish line of success. When you can conquer yourself, you can truly conquer anything. It's a matter of personal conditioning of the mind, body, and soul for business success. You can do it. Again, it's just a matter of how badly you want it. I was passionate about running and completing that marathon. You must be passionate about your entrepreneurial endeavor. That passion will fuel your desire to cross the finish line no matter what.

## Always be learning

With all of the resources available to us, a lack of knowledge is no excuse for not getting the job done. We live in the information age. Want to learn something? Just Google it. You can find a blog, article, podcast, video, magazine, or book that will teach you everything you ever need to know about the subject you're interested in.

Successful people are lifelong learners. They realize that there is always more information to be consumed and that the world is always changing. Investing in yourself can enhance your skills and competency, helping you become more efficient and effective at growing your enterprise. As we were taught in school, knowledge is power.

I recommend spending a little time each day reading. There are so many great books out there on every aspect of growing a business. Set aside an hour each day and read. Get in a quiet place where no one is going to bother you, where you won't be distracted, and just read. Have a notebook handy, because you're going to learn things that you can use to grow your business.

Another thing you can do is become a great networker. Some of the best things I've ever learned came by talking to others. I promise that there are networking events for entrepreneurs in your area, and with the popularity of social networking, you can also connect with other business owners online and learn from them without even leaving your home.

## Get organized and focused

When you're disorganized, you're going to make costly mistakes. That's all there is to it. The good news is that it's actually pretty easy to get organized, so you can work smarter, not harder:

- **Clean up your desk**—In a 2010 survey conducted by the National Association of Professional Organizers and Office Depot, out of more than 1,000 office workers surveyed, 82 percent said they feel being organized improved their performance; however, 32 percent admitted their workspace was disorganized and 42 percent said they only clean up their workspace once a month or less. A cluttered workspace causes a cluttered mind. An entrepreneur already has enough chaos to deal with as it is. Don't make the problem worse by having a chaotic workspace. Clean up and get it organized.

- **Use only one calendar**—Find a calendar that works for you, and stick with it. Whether it's on your computer, your project management tool, your phone, or a physical calendar in your office, pick one calendar and stick with it. Get rid of every other calendar, and just use one to keep track of everything. Otherwise, you'll get confused and forget important deadlines.

- **Set goals**—Make a list of specific goals you want to achieve in your business this year. Be as specific as you can, and have dates. Whether your goal is to make a certain amount of money or build your client base to a certain number, it's up to you. Setting goals helps you stay focused on what's really important in your business. Anything that's not contributing to you reaching those goals shouldn't be a priority.

- **Update your contact list**—On a schedule that works for you, go through your contact list (we called it a rolodex back in the day now it's my MS Outlook). Clear it out and make sure you keep it up to date. Your prioritized contacts and the relationships they represent are important to your business. Keeping them active and lively can provide opportunities and prevent lost time later by ensuring they are responsive.

- **Organize your business documents**—Keep all of your official business documents centralized in one place, and index them so that you can easily find them whenever you need them. If your office is paperless, make sure you avoid digital clutter by having a smart file organization strategy on your computer(s) – and backup everything of importance regularly. For emails, use the single-touch approach. That means, either respond to it, file it, or delete it the first time you read it.

- **Keep a time journal**—For some this might be the most important thing you could do. If you keep track of your time, you can see exactly what it is that you're really doing with your work days. Get a journal, and every task you do, write it down. If you spend 30 minutes making business calls, write it down. If you waste 45 minutes on Facebook, write that down. When you put it in writing, you can easily see if you're wasting time or spending time on nonessential tasks.

- **Reserve time and space for working on your business**—Keep a consistent scheduled block of time in each day that is reserved just for working on your business. This time should be focused only on achieving the important items for the welfare of the business. As I said, this time management is one of the most important things you can do. In addition, keep a separate space that is dedicated to the work of the business. Eliminate distractions from it as much as possible. No TV. No kids running around. Just you and your business.

## Learn how to multitask

While there are certain tasks that you'll do that require your complete, undivided attention (such as handling payroll or reviewing a contract), there are many other daily tasks that lend themselves to multitasking, saving you time and energy. Remember, you're going to be wearing many different hats, so you have to get good at juggling several things at once.

Want to be an effective multi-tasker? Here are some simple tips to help you out:

- Keep a notebook handy to write down all tasks that need to be done, ensuring you don't forget anything.

- Make a prioritized to-do list for yourself each morning. It only takes a few minutes for you to do, and you can check off tasks throughout the day as you complete them, helping you stay focused.

- Use the latest tools and apps to help you get more done. Whatever works best for you, from MS Outlook Calendar to online calendars hosted on the cloud to Google Reader for bookmarking interesting, helpful websites, there are tons of great tools that help entrepreneurs multitask and be more productive. There are also great smartphone apps (mine is Android) that you can download for free or minimal cost from their online store that will provide you with one integrated source of calendars, memos, email, voicemail, GPS, and more. It's like having an office in the palm of your hand.

- When you get stuck, don't be afraid to take a quick break. Do what for you clears and re-energizes your mind. Sometimes I will take short power naps (more on this later) when I need to accomplish this.

## Get help to lighten the load

Successful entrepreneurs have a keen understanding of their strengths and weaknesses. They realize that they may lack skills and knowledge in certain areas, so they surround themselves with smart, qualified people who can pick up the slack.

Even when they don't necessarily lack the skills or knowledge to get a particular task done, they know when their time would be better spent working on something else, and they hire someone to complete the task.

Let's go back to my analogy of how building a business is like building a house. Think of how hard it would be to build a house on your own. It would take years! You'd probably get so overloaded that you'd eventually give up because it was just too hard to do on your own.

Now imagine building a house alongside a team of experienced carpenters, electricians, plumbers, and designers. It's starting to sound a little easier now, isn't it? You'd get the job done more quickly, and the house would look and function better because you surrounded yourself with talented people who could handle the various tasks that needed to be done.

This same concept applies to building your business. You might not be able to do it all on your own. Smart entrepreneurs understand this, so they partner with and hire people that have the skills, knowledge, and experience to help them grow their business.

Of course, the hardest parts are admitting you need help and giving up control by delegating responsibility to others. But if you can't learn to do these things, you're severely limiting your chances of success.

Of course, you have to choose wisely which tasks you'll handle yourself and which you'll outsource. I recommend spending your time on tasks that are directly related to running and growing your business. I'm talking about things like business strategy, sales, and reviewing operating expenses.

There are all sorts of other tasks you can outsource. For example, you can get a virtual assistant or contractor to help with some tasks as errands or research you need for planning your business. Another example of a task you should hand off to someone else is the design of your website and marketing materials. You don't need to be wasting your precious time and energy on tasks that are not the best use of your focus and talents.

## Make time for your personal life

Over the course of my career thus far, I've developed businesses, teams, and individuals, coaching them to success. I've helped entrepreneurs launch successful startups, and I've assisted Fortune 500 companies in transforming their businesses. I've helped businesses gain benefits from thousands of dollars to hundreds of millions. I've done this while traveling across the world on business.

But the thing I'm most proud of?

My greatest achievements are being a husband, father, and friend. I say this without any doubt in my mind.

Make no mistake. Being an entrepreneur is going to have an effect on your personal life. But it's up to you to make sure that it doesn't wreck your personal life. Yes, you will have to make some sacrifices, but you can't completely abandon your personal life. You must make time for family, friends, hobbies, and love.

Believe me, no one ever lies on their deathbed wishing that they had closed another deal or worked another hour. People lie on their deathbed wishing that they had spent more time doing the things that truly mattered in life, spending time with the people they love. It was most striking to me when I read that in Steve Jobs' last months and weeks he made it a priority to get home and have dinner with his family each day. He was a tremendously successful entrepreneur but also had a successful marriage and family.

The best advice I can give you is to find ways to create boundaries between your work and personal life. This is especially important for entrepreneurs who work at home, because it's so easy for the boundaries to blur; and when that happens, both your work and personal lives can suffer.

Boundaries are essential. For example, when you're spending time with your kids, really spend time with them. Don't check your email. Turn your phone off altogether, as a matter of fact, and really focus on talking to them, playing with them, watching their ball games, or just relaxing with them while watching TV. Quality time really does count. Don't even let yourself think about work during these times. It will actually make you more productive when you do focus on the business.

Another tip I'd like to offer is to not check your email right before you go to sleep at night. I know it's tempting to grab your smart phone off the night stand, and check your work email, but don't do it. You don't want your brain to try to go from entrepreneur to sleep mode in just a few seconds. Checking email right before bed can make it difficult for the mind to wind down for sleep. You have to let yourself go to sleep and wake up gradually and enjoy a few quiet moments without thinking about work. Trust me; it will do wonders for you.

Most of all, just protect your "you" time. This is the time where you get away from it all and decompress. Find something that you love to do...something that makes you feel relaxed and like you don't have a care in the world. For me, it's things like fishing and golf. Also, when I make time for prayer in the mornings before starting my day, it settles my emotions, removes anxiety, and clears my mind. When I'm fishing or golfing, all of my work-related worries are pushed out of my mind, I'm at peace with myself, and I get recharged. Nothing puts a smile on my face like a big fish pulling on my line. I know of others who use yoga, rock climbing, exercise...you name it...to help them get away from it all. Find your escape.

I know, I know, you were thinking I'd be harping on how to work harder and longer so to squeeze out the last drop of work, but really, some of the things I mention in this chapter that you may not have expected can make you more productive (and happy) when you're at work.

## Protect your sleep

Earlier, I mentioned that you might want to get used to not sleeping as much, and that will be true at times for some entrepreneurs. That means the meager amount of sleep that you do get is all the more important. You must protect this sleep at all costs!

I'm most productive after I get some good sleep, but sleeping eight hours a night just isn't always possible. That's why I take power naps sometimes in the day. Any time I'm feeling dull and unproductive, I take a quick nap and *viola!*...a solution to whatever issue I'm working through usually comes to my mind.

It's all about quality over quantity where your sleep is concerned. If you can't get a lot of sleep, at least make sure that the sleep you do get is great, undisturbed sleep. Learn your biorhythms and how to manage yourself for the best personal productivity.

## Eat smart

If you're fueling your body with a bunch of junk, it's not going to run the way it should. You'll always be tired and unproductive. If you put contaminated gas in your auto, it will sputter. I'm no dietician, but I do know from years of personal experience that I'm far more productive after eating a healthy meal than I am when I scarf down some fast food or vending machine fare. Provide your bodily engine with good, quality fuel.

Now, I know that when you're working long days and you have almost no time to stop and eat that it's more convenient to grab a quick bite at the local burger joint or a snack from the vending machine down the hall. But at these moments it can make a difference if the effort is made to make smart eating decisions. Either pack a healthy lunch or if you have to go out, opt for the local sandwich shop instead of the burger shack.

I also highly recommend taking quality vitamins daily. Go down to your local drug store or health food store and find a good multivitamin. Your body will get many of the nutrients that it needs, helping you stay energetic and productive.

## Get adequate exercise

When you're working long days and evenings, the last thing you feel like doing is working out. I get it, believe me, but there are so many benefits to exercising regularly that I believe ever entrepreneur needs to do it. When you exercise a few times a week, you will:

- Have more energy to get things done through the day

- Burn off the stress that comes with being an entrepreneur

- Feel more awake and alert

- Sleep better at night

- Be healthier and miss less time at work from being sick

My experience has been that if one makes exercising convenient, they will do so more. Yet it has not worked for me to have exercise equipment in the home. There is a great fitness center 10 minutes from my home office. This combination of out of the house but close by is great for me. Get the right setup for you so you can ensure adequate exercise and realize these benefits. It can make you more productive for your business, and add to the quality of your life.

## Monitor your TV time

According to A.C. Nielsen Co., the average American spends more than four hours a day watching TV. That's two months each year. In a 65-year life, that person will have wasted nine years on the couch watching TV. Isn't there something better and more productive for your business you could be doing with that kind of time?

Look, I'm not saying not to watch TV. It's nice to plop down on the couch and relax while getting your news or just enjoying some mindless entertainment, but this is an area that one could pay attention to and redeem some valuable time. Even spending an hour less watching TV each day could make a significant difference in productivity.

## Work with a professional mentor

If you're really serious about getting more done with your time, you should consider investing in a professional business advisor. When you work with a mentor, you get access to their experience, knowledge, and methods that will help you be more productive and reach goals that you may not be able to reach on your own. You could also prevent mistakes and keep yourself from wasting time by heading in the wrong direction.

A good business advisor will help you:

- Discover your strengths and opportunities to benefit

- Develop your personalized success strategy

- Make a plan that works for you

- Obtain resources that empower you

- Support your growth

If you have further interest in entrepreneurial mentoring and coaching you can discover more at:

www.successfulentrepreneuradvisor.com.

"Effort only fully releases its reward after a person refuses to quit."

~ Napoleon Hill

# 6

## HOW TO OVERCOME BARRIER #3: DIFFICULTY IN RAISING CAPITAL

"Capital as such is not evil; it is its wrong use that is evil. Capital in some form or other will always be needed."

~ Mahatma Gandhi

When Karen Mills, the head of the U.S. Small Business Administration, was asked in an AP interview what the greatest challenge small business owners faced was, her answer was clear: "access to capital."

Over the past several years, we've seen credit markets freeze due to imbalances and severe recession in the economy. Those looking to fund a new business venture through conventional channels have found it more difficult than before to get the money needed to get a business off the ground.

Just ask Eric Migicovsky, the founder of Pebble, a startup that manufactures wristwatches that display information from an iPhone or Android, such as text messages, caller ID, music playlists, alerts, and more. When Migicovsky tried going the traditional routes of raising capital to finance his company, he had no luck. He couldn't secure any money to fund the Pebble watch. He was forced to think outside the box and explore new avenues to raise capital, but it wasn't easy. More on that a little later, though.

The point is this – starting a new business costs money. Depending on the type of business you're starting, it could cost anywhere from a few thousand dollars well into the millions. You need money to cover things like leasing office/retail space, buying equipment, hiring contractors, paying employees, advertising your company, and a whole host of other expenses. And that doesn't even include the capital you'll need if your business takes a little longer to start turning a profit than you initially predicted.

It's like people always say, it takes money to make money.

It doesn't matter what your current business situation is. Whether you simply have a great idea for a new venture or you've already been in business for years, you'll usually welcome an infusion of funds with open arms.

Of course, money doesn't grow on trees. And without a sound financial plan to execute your ideas, your business will never materialize or it will never reach its full potential. It will simply either remain as ideas or as an underperforming business that eventually dies out.

The reality is that most entrepreneurs struggle to find a way to get the capital they need to build their business. In fact, some 91% of entrepreneurs surveyed admitted that difficulty in raising capital was an important inhibitor that prevents many from starting their own businesses.

Now, I'm not here to tell you that raising money for your venture will be a piece of cake, and I'm not going to tell you that you won't run into any problems in your quest for capital. But I do believe that the biggest reason entrepreneurs struggle with raising capital is a simple lack of knowledge. The money is out there to be had if you have a good reason for it, like a good new idea, unique talents, new product or approaches. You just have to know how to get it.

With that in mind, this section will explore the financial issues entrepreneurs face when trying to get a company off the ground. This section is intended to provide information that will increase your odds of success in obtaining the capital you need to finally turn that great idea you have into an actual business. It's my hope that this chapter will provide you with helpful, practical advice that you can use in building your blueprint to conquer the immense challenge of funding your business.

I'm going to tell you some of the challenges entrepreneurs run into when trying to raise capital, some common mistakes they make (and how to avoid them), and what you can consider in achieving success raising capital for your business.

So let's look at where entrepreneurs typically receive their capital from.

## Major Sources of Funding: What They Are & How to Use Them

### *Personal savings and assets*

In the Kauffman survey of entrepreneurs, 70% of serial entrepreneurs said they used personal savings as a main source of funding for their first business. This is more than four times the number chiefly financed by any other type of funding. Furthermore, more than 50% of these entrepreneurs used their personal savings to finance future ventures.

The authors of *Raising Entrepreneurial Capital* put it bluntly, "The first person to turn to for capital is yourself. Before approaching others, the entrepreneur should exhaust his or her personal sources of capital."

The authors go on to state that of the CEOs who made the 2002 Inc. 500 list, 87% used personal assets to start their business. Obviously, this is the preferable approach and most traveled path by budding entrepreneurs. You avoid debt and don't lose control or focus as you would when bringing in other investors.

Did you know Dell, a Fortune 500 Company that was at one time the largest seller of personal computers and servers in the world, was started out of a dorm room with founder Michael Dell's $1,000 in personal savings?

It's true. Dell took $1,000 out of his savings account and started building and selling computers for people he knew at college. He focused on building great machines at the lowest prices possible. Before long, he had customers outside of his school, and during Dell's first full year in business, he had generated $6 million in sales. Sixteen years later, Dell was a billionaire with offices around the world.

And he did all of this with just a great idea, a smart business strategy, and only $1,000 in personal savings. And Dell isn't alone in its radical transformation from a company with humble beginnings to a massive success. There are countless success stories of companies that were started with very little—Wrigley, Apple, Nordstrom, Mattel, Starbucks, eBay…the list is very long and it's always growing. There's nothing to stop you from creating your own similar success story!

Now, there are many ways you can personally finance your startup. These include:

- **Tap into actual personal savings**—If you've been smart with your money, you may have a nest egg stowed away to use for various reasons as retirement, covering unexpected expenses on a rainy day, or just to have a little fun when the time is right. While most entrepreneurs use personal savings as a source for startup financing, there is little information out there on how much of your personal savings you should use. Should you empty out your savings account? Use half of it? Even less. What's the smart move? Let me say this—it's never a good idea to use all of your personal savings. Doing so can leave you and your family in a precarious situation should any emergency expenses arise. You don't want to get in a situation where you've completely run out of money and you desperately have to borrow money just to get by. I recommend that you keep a reserve amount that you are comfortable with in your personal savings that you consider a line you will not violate. Not only will this help protect you and your family, but it could also prove to be a valuable decision point for you relative to your business. If you ever get to a point that you've run out of money and are considering tapping into that reserve, you'll be forced to really evaluate your options. Should you tap into these reserves to create a quick cash infusion for your business? Should you look elsewhere for capital? Is your business really viable?

- **Sell your assets**—Take a look around you. I'm betting you own a few things that are worth some money—a boat, second properties, additional vehicles, jewelry, antiques...the list goes on and on. These are all assets you can sell to help raise capital for your business. Of course, it's up to you. How badly do you really want to get your business off the ground? Do you want it bad enough to depart with some of the nice things you've acquired during your life? Now, I will say this. When selling your assets to raise money, it can be very easy to get caught up and sell off a lot, often times at prices far below the item's true value. Don't treat this like you're going to a pawn shop for a quick payday. Make sure you're getting a fair value for your assets, and never sell those truly irreplaceable items (e.g. heirlooms and possessions that have sentimental value).

- **Borrow against your home**—According to the New York Times, "the percentage of small business owners who tapped their home equity for business, either by pledging their homes as collateral or by borrowing against home equity, rose to 27.5 percent from 18.4 percent." Entrepreneurs have long been betting the house as a way to help their businesses grow. The way they usually do it is to legally pledge equity they have in their home to the financial institution as collateral for the loan. Let's say your business needs $20,000, and your home is worth $150,000, but you still owe the bank $100,000 on your mortgage. In this case, you have $50,000 in equity that you may be able borrow against. The success of doing this and wisdom of putting your residence at risk depends on factors as the borrower's credit worthiness, cash flow and ability to repay, and the value you can add to the business with these funds. Now, you'll have to make monthly payments on this loan, so if possible and necessary it's smart to set aside some of the proceeds from your home equity loan to help cover these payments until your business produces steady cash flow to cover this additional expense.

- **Borrow against your life insurance policy**—If you've had a whole life policy for a number of years, it could have some cash value by now. You could get in touch with your agent or insurance company, and let them know that you want a policy loan. As a general rule of thumb, some insurance companies could lend up to 90% of the cash value of the whole life policy, and you'll still have your policy intact as long as you keep paying the premiums. Something to keep in mind though is that typically the benefits of the policy are diminished until the loan is repaid. Yet on the positive side usually the financial terms such as interest rate on such a loan against an insurance policy are comparatively favorable.

- **Charge it on your credit card**—Okay, so it's not the most creative way to get a quick infusion of capital, but plastic has been used to jumpstart many a business. Of course, credit card debt has also brought down many an entrepreneur, so you have to use credit cards cautiously. Sky-high interest rates can have you buried over your head in debt in no time at all if you're reckless.

Some suggestions?

First of all, if possible make sure you keep your personal and business credit cards separate. It's professional, ensures proper accounting, and if the legal structure of the business is done properly it could possibly prevent business debt from going against your personal credit history and assets. You also have to be careful not to go crazy and get as many cards and as much credit as you can. Just because you can get the credit doesn't mean you should take it. Use one or two credit cards at the most, and carefully track your expenses. Finally, make sure you know your credit history because that's going to play a huge role in determining whether or not you qualify for a credit card (or any other type of loan, for that matter) and what your interest rate will be. There are many different services out there that will give you access so to manage ongoing your credit scores and reports at reasonable cost. Educate yourself so that you're not surprised later on.

- **Work a side job**—When you have a great business idea, it can be really tempting to drop everything and put all your time and energy into building your new business. But for a lot of people, this just isn't realistic. Many people can't afford to quit their jobs and gamble everything on their new business. They have families to support and mouths to feed, so they can't put themselves in such a risky predicament. But just because you're not able to quit your job doesn't mean that you can't start building your new business. In fact, if you continue to work at your job or get a side job, you can use some of your pay as financing for your new venture. This way, you'll have steady pay coming in while you focus on getting your business running to the point that it's bringing in enough money that you can eventually quit your job and work on your business full time.

A few words of advice to consider about working a side job in starting your own business:

  o Make sure you know your employer's policy about other employment. Some employers may see you starting your own business as a conflict of interest, so you need to be knowledgeable in this and prepare accordingly.

o Be careful freely talking about your venture at work. It could be seen as a distraction, and you could be putting a bull's-eye on your back and possibly on your venture.

o Resist the temptation to involve others you work with. You might think a co-worker would be a perfect fit for your new venture, but if you plan on keeping your job for a while, don't recruit your co-workers since it could draw undesirable attention from your employer.

o Don't quit your job too early. Remember, you're working this job because you need funding for your new venture. It can take a while to get a new business to the point that it's consistently turning a profit, so stay the course until your business is truly consistent.

When using your personal funds for financing your business, a main thing to remember is that all sources of personal debt can add to your cash flow troubles and your stress. Using personal savings and assets can be wise and helpful, but always be cautious that you don't overextend yourself and put yourself at an amount of risk that you're not prepared to handle.

### *Venture capital and angel investors*

First-time entrepreneurs don't often seek funding from venture capital and angel investors. It is difficult, and most entrepreneurs are not successful in this path to capital. In the Kauffman study, just 11% of entrepreneurs received venture capital for their first business and 9% received angel financing. But as entrepreneurs launch subsequent businesses, they become likelier to take venture and angel funding, with "26% and 22%, respectively, of entrepreneur's most recent startups receiving such funding." Having demonstrated cash flow and some degree of past success better positions you.

Pitching venture capital investors to launch or grow your business is a very delicate task that requires a carefully planned approach. Make no mistake about it, there's an art to pitching venture capital investors and angel investors successfully.

To give yourself the best shot with investors, consider these helpful tips:

- **Research potential venture capitalists carefully—** Many entrepreneurs make the mistake of blindly reaching out to potential investors with a generic pitch. This kills their chances of getting funded. Remember, every venture capitalist is different. Each investor has different types of companies they like to invest in, different things they want to see when analyzing potential investments, and different amounts of money they are willing to put up. That's why you need to spend time researching the investors you plan to pitch. Look at the types of companies they have invested in and pay attention to what stage the companies are in when they make their investments. For example, if a venture capitalist tends to only invest in established companies looking to grow, you probably would be wasting your time pitching your startup to them.

- **Prove why your idea is great**—Having an amazing idea for a business is only a small part of the battle. You need to prove to potential investors that your idea can actually succeed as a real business. That means having a well-written, realistic business strategy and business case that emphasizes your sustainable competitive advantage and strategy for executing your idea successfully. According to the Small Business Administration, businesses with a plan are 40% more likely to survive than businesses without a plan. However, 60% of small businesses do not have a written business plan. Having researched and thought it through thoroughly until you could document it convincingly makes a difference in success or failure. Even better, already having demonstrable business results to support your pitch makes it much more compelling providing a better opportunity for winning venture capital. This could come from efforts while already executing on your business strategy and business case when exploring and evolving your business idea with methods such as business prototyping and market probing. Of course having actually launched and run the business for some period of time while recording cash flow is even better.

- **Be prepared to answer questions...lots of them—** Venture capitalists and angel investors aren't just going to hand you money without doing their due diligence. They are going to have a lot of questions, and they'll probably stop you in the middle of your presentation to ask them. These are smart and experienced business people who will typically know within a few minutes of your presentation whether they want to listen and know more. So be flexible and prepared to answer their questions as succinctly as possible. Being well-prepared is very important, it will enable you to make sure you're having a conversation with the investors when answering their questions and not seem to be just spitting out your rehearsed pitch.

- **Be realistic**—You might truly believe that you're going to be the next Mark Zuckerberg (the founder of Facebook), and maybe you will, but no venture capitalist or angel investor wants to hear an unrealistic pitch. You have to put away the rose tinted shades and be unbiased and realistic when making your pitch. Demonstrate that you've put in the research and testing of your business, industry, and competitors, and clearly outline your strategy for success with a sound business case and clear facts.

### *Family and friends*

Some entrepreneurs turn to friends and family for funding. It's one of the oldest methods of raising capital in the book. In fact, 16% of entrepreneurs in the Kauffman survey received funding from friends and family.

An Inc. Magazine article stated that, "investments by family and friends account for more than 70% of all venture dollars for start-ups, according to a recent study by Babson College, the London Business School, and the Kauffman Foundation."

In fact, Whole Foods Market, a wildly successful chain of grocery stores and a Fortune 500 Company, was started in 1978 by John Mackey (a college dropout) and Rene Lawson Hardy (a 21-year old) with their personal savings and money borrowed from family and friends.

Within their first year of business, Mackey and Hardy were evicted from their apartment for using it as storage for their inventory. They were homeless, but they didn't give up. Instead, they decided to save money by living in their store. The two bathed using a Hobart dishwasher!

But guess what? Here we are over 30 years later, and Whole Foods Market now has more than 310 stores across the United States, Canada, and the United Kingdom. The Fortune 500 Company posts billions in revenue each year and shows no signs of slowing its growth.

But here's something to remember. Borrowing money from family members and friends can end in disaster. Family gatherings can see dinners turn into shareholder's meetings, and if your business fails and others lose money, you could quickly become a pariah who can't go to social gatherings without a nasty incident occurring.

But there are ways to avoid problems when borrowing from family and friends:

- **Do your homework before asking for money**—One of the common mistakes entrepreneurs make is to get overly excited about their idea and ask friends and family for money immediately. They do this before developing a formal business strategy and business case without really putting in the research and analysis that's necessary to determine if the idea can truly be turned into a successful venture. You must treat your friends and families with the same respect you would a banker or venture capitalist. Supply them with realistic financial projections, a clear strategy for building your business, and an honest assessment of when they will be paid back.

- **Figure out the arrangement that makes sense for you**—There are two basic kinds of arrangements you can make when tapping friends and family for capital:

1) Take out a loan from them that you'll repay later

2) Offer them equity in your company.

A preference would be taking out a low interest loan from family members and friends rather than making them partners in your business. Why? You don't want to get yourself in a situation where friends and family are trying to tell you how to run the business.

- **Don't have too many lenders or investors**—Not only does it increasingly dilute your ownership and profit, but when you have too many lenders or investors, you have a lot of different relationships and expectations that you have to manage. These relationships take a lot of time…time that could be spent running your business. This is especially true if you give your friends and family a stake in your company. The more investors you have, the more difficult for everyone to agree on how the business should be run and how profits should be distributed. Ever heard the expression "too many cooks in the kitchen?"

- **Get everything in writing**—When you take out a loan from a bank or get an investment from a venture capital firm, there's a lot of paperwork that has to be completed and signed. You need to take this same professional approach when seeking capital from friends and family. Having everything in writing prevents any misunderstandings or "I said, he said" arguments later on.

## *Banks*

Of the entrepreneurs surveyed in the Kauffman study, 16% turned to banks to get funding for their most recent startups. But thanks to the recent economic collapse and the changing landscape of U.S. small firms from manufacturers to service companies with little to no collateral, getting a bank loan is harder than ever before.

Note that I said it's harder than ever before. I didn't say it was impossible.

When turning to banks for business capital, stick to these tips to give yourself better chances of success:

- **Educate the lender**—Whether you're seeking lending from a large financial institution or a local community bank, you should expect that the representative of the lender usually doesn't know as much about your industry and business as you do. Any lack of knowledge and understanding of your industry and business can cause apprehension and hesitation about granting the loan. Your job is to educate the lender on your industry, and your business. This includes utilizing the same approaches as previously mentioned for investors. Talk about the important factors in your industry (e.g. technology, cyclicality, seasonality, competitive landscape, trends, opportunities, etc.) so that the lender can have a better understanding of the environment your business will be operating in. Present your strategy and business case with your results thus far. Convincingly educate them that you're a good investment.

- **Beware of predatory lenders**—Because banks are being tighter with their loans than ever before, many have turned to riskier financing alternatives. A recent CNN article details how many entrepreneurs have started to turn to cash advance companies that offer quick money at exorbitant interest rates. The article states that, "Those in the trade...offer quick money with a hefty fee. Typical clients are restaurants and small shops, which take out advances that range between $5,000 and $200,000. A business owner who takes out a $70,000 advance will have to pay back $100,000. Lenders ensure repayment by immediately taking a fixed portion, close to 15%, of a sale every time a customer swipes a credit card at the shop." The loans come easy, and I can see how tempting to take out a cash advance when in a bind, but I strongly suggest that if taking out one of these loans, absolutely make sure the situation demands it and you have exhausted other more appropriate sources of capital. This should be your last resort for raising capital. Beware of easy money and protect yourself.

- **Know the risks and have a plan for mitigating them—** Lenders want to know the risks associated with your industry and business. You can't hide these risks. They will find out, and if you aren't upfront about these risks and proactive in explaining your strategy for mitigating or eliminating these risks, you won't get the loan. It's that simple. Your goal is to give your lender confidence that you know how to manage these risks effectively. You must demonstrate that you know what you are doing and are truly prepared to face these risks should you get the loan.

- **Don't forget credit unions and community banks—** Many entrepreneurs find it difficult to get a loan from the megabanks, like Chase, Bank of America, and Wells Fargo. That's why entrepreneurs often turn to local credit unions and community banks to apply for a small business loan. Smaller financial institutions are often a bit more flexible and personable in their lending practices, whereas the megabanks have very tight, rigid criteria that must be met for getting a loan.

## *Factoring*

A lot of startups struggle with cash flow issues. On paper, they might appear to be profitable, but due to slow paying clients or long invoice processing periods, they struggle having enough cash on hand to keep the business up and running.

Factoring is a capital generating technique used by companies facing cash flow problems. Here's how it works: A business sells its invoices or accounts receivable to a third party company (called a "factor") at a discount, which could vary from 5 to 30%. The factoring party who has expertise in collections then advances the majority of the invoice amount to the business after verifying the credit worthiness of the billed customer. Once that billed customer pays the invoice, the factor sends the remaining balance to the business, minus a processing (or factoring) fee.

There can be variations on the factoring approach that are determined by the agreement between the business and the factoring party. The variables could be relative to items as discounts, fees, timing, and recourse. Obviously, one must carefully read the contractual agreement to understand if the terms are something they can accept.

In other words, factoring allows you to see some of that money your customers owe you much more quickly, but in the end, it has costs which can add up when paying fees to the factor for advancing you the funds. It's a tradeoff. This fee could also be substantial because the factor knows how badly you need the money. It's kind of like those companies who offer payday loans to people who need cash now. They charge exorbitant interest fees for giving a customer a payday advance. Factors may charge several percentage points more than a typical lender, but it does have its benefits.

When you have an account where payment isn't due from the customer for another number of days but you need cash right now to make payroll or to keep the lights on at your business, factoring can be a pretty attractive option. Also, if you've explored other financing options without any success, factoring may be the only option that you have left. If you don't have the money and no other lenders are willing to give it to you, turning to a factor might be your next best move.

Some entrepreneurs actually prefer working with factors because they don't require all of the paperwork and cutting through red tape that comes with banks and other investors. This is due to it being a different type of financial transaction—one is a purchase by the factor based on the value of your business receivables, and the other is a loan from a bank based on the value of your assets they use as collateral. In addition, using a factor allows the entrepreneur to hand off the task of collections, meaning he or she no longer has to spend time chasing down customers to get them to pay or staffing for this important task.

Typically, those who use factoring do so as a stop-gap measure. The high fees charged by factors make it an unwise financing choice for long-term use, but if you're in a pinch and nothing else is working exploring factoring options could make sense.

## Crowd funding

Call it trendy or a fad if you want, but if you ask me, crowd funding could be the way of the future. Heck, it's a part of the way of the now.

What is crowd funding?

It's a new, innovative way to raise capital. Using a crowd funding platform (some popular ones include Kickstarter, IndieGoGo, Fundable, and Rockethub), an entrepreneur posts a description of his or her venture, provides an outline of the business plan, tells the amount of capital needed, and explains what the contributor will receive in return for contributing money to the cause.

Thanks to Title III of the JOBS Act signed into place in April 2012, businesses are now allowed to raise small amounts of equity capital through crowd funding without having to register with the SEC (equity funding used to be expensive due to SEC filing requirements).

Remember Eric Migicovsky, the founder of Pebble watches mentioned earlier in this chapter? When he struggled to raise capital through traditional means, he turned to Kickstarter, perhaps the most popular crowd funding outlet.

His project stated that everyone who contributed $99 to fund the venture would receive a Pebble watch in return once they were manufactured. Within two hours of posting the project, Migicovsky and his partners hit their goal of $100,000. That same night, they hit $600,000, and by the time all was said and done, they had raised $10 million. Needless to say, the company exceeded its modest goal of $100,000 by quite a bit!

But Migicovsky is far from the only entrepreneur to find success raising capital with crowd funding. There are many success stories, from singer Amanda Palmer raising more than $1 million to record a new album to Tim Schafer raking in nearly $3.5 million to develop a video game.

Of course, crowd funding isn't a tactic that's guaranteed to be successful for all entrepreneurs. Sure, it makes raising capital easier than before, but it's still not easy. People aren't just going to give you money because you ask for it – you have to earn it by convincing them that your project is worth funding.

Here are a few tips for crowd funding success:

- **Have a strong plan**—It doesn't matter who it is that you're asking for money, they're going to want to see that you have a good plan for the money before they'll give it to you. That means you need to do your homework and come up with a strong plan for your business. You need to truly put your business idea through the paces to verify that it can work, identify potential challenges and risks, and come up with a clear strategy for bringing your idea to life as a successful business. Make your case clearly and compellingly.

- **Be honest about the risks**—Not only is it the right thing to do morally, but now it's required by Kickstarter (and other crowd funding outlets) that you outline all of the risks and challenges of your project. Kickstarter added this requirement after donors started getting frustrated when the projects they contributed to didn't pan out like they were led to believe they would. So, you have to be very clear and upfront about any risks associated with your venture.

- **Be smart about what you'll give up in return**—With crowd funding, you give investors something in return for their contribution. Some companies offer products developed, others offer experiences or access, and even others offer merchandise goodies. You have to be smart about what you're willing to give up in return for funding. Yes, you might really need that money right now to get your venture up and running, but if you promise something in return make sure you can deliver that without putting yourself in a risky position, or you could wind up in a bad situation. Above all else, make sure you protect and stay in control of your company.

- **Be clear about the terms of the transaction**—Investors need to know exactly what they're getting for their money. Establish these guidelines up front, telling people what the price is, what they get in return, and what their rights are now and in the future as an investor.

- **Keep the momentum up**—Crowd funding campaigns have a tendency to be hot for a while before going stale and losing all their steam. You need to have a plan in place for keeping the momentum going and attracting investors over the duration of the campaign. I recommend trying to build buzz before launching your campaign so that you have people ready to jump onboard once it goes live, and then, try to schedule exciting news and updates throughout your campaign to keep people excited and motivated to give.

## *Microfinancing*

When you think of microloans, you might have visions of poor people in developing countries starting their own businesses thanks to small loans from a nonprofit group. While that might have been the face of microlending in times past, it's not anymore. The truth is that microfinancing has found a comfortable home right here in the United States.

Microloans have traditionally been designed to help low-income entrepreneurs get started, and this is still the case today as microlending has become more commonplace in the United States. Entrepreneurs who have a solid business idea but lack the income to get it off the ground can apply for microfinancing—a small loan with reasonable interest rates and minimum requirements to qualify.

Of course, not every entrepreneur can get a microloan.

Microloans are typically awarded to:

- Low-income entrepreneurs

- Entrepreneurs working in disadvantaged communities

- Entrepreneurs with poor credit

And it's important to note that microfinancing is typically much more than just helping an entrepreneur raise capital. The process often involves extensive business counseling, teaching the new entrepreneur how to best go about starting a business and how to run it on a day-to-day basis to increase its chances of success. Think of it as relationship-based funding for entrepreneurs and small businesses.

The success stories of microfinancing are growing daily and a favorite is the story of Fauzia Abdur-Rahman. When she was 20 years old, she visited New York City on vacation. She ended up staying here, and after working for social services for eight years, decided to start her own business so she could enjoy greater flexibility to spend time with her children and provide for them.

For 16 years, Fauzia operated a food cart near Yankee Stadium, working from morning until late at night. The work was hard and uncomfortable, so Fauzia decided to upgrade her cart, but she needed financing. The loan she needed was too small for most lenders to consider, but thanks to microfinancing, she was able to buy her new food cart with a loan from ACCION USA. Today, her food cart is more popular than ever before, she was even featured in the *Daily News* –a popular New York newspaper, and now her food carts and locations are expanding.

This is just one of the stories that highlights the real difference microfinance is making here in America and all across the world. It's a real movement that is helping produce a whole new crop of brilliant entrepreneurs who are contributing to the economy, making better lives for themselves and their loved ones, and inspiring people everywhere to chase their dreams against all odds.

Personally, I love the microfinancing movement. It's what America is all about—giving everyone the chance to succeed and chase the American Dream. I love seeing budding entrepreneurs who wouldn't be able to get loans from banks, wouldn't be able to get their foot in the door at a venture capital firm, and just don't have the money to finance their own business finally get the chance to unleash their inner entrepreneur and have a real shot at making it.

If interested in opportunities for a microloan thinking you may qualify, you could look into the following: SBA Microloan Program, Kiva, ACCION USA, and Communities at Work Fund. You can also find microfinance information at websites as www.microfinancegateway.org and www.microenterpriseworks.org.

### Additional Considerations on Raising Capital

Before we conclude this section on raising capital for your business, I'd like to share a few more items for you to consider.

### *Keep costs down by taking advantage of technology*

The fact is that raising money is difficult for most entrepreneurs. While you can certainly have success exploring the avenues previously mentioned in this chapter, I suggest developing a less capital-intensive business model, so you can finance the startup yourself rather than spending every waking moment trying to raise money from others.

The good news is that it has never been cheaper to start a business than it is right now. Thanks to the easy accessibility of low-cost, high-value technology, anyone can easily setup a home office and launch a profitable business without the need to fight tooth and nail to raise startup capital.

Take a look at eBay, the world's most popular auction website. The company was started out of a living room by French-born Iranian immigrant Pierre Omidyar. The eBay founder took advantage of technology by coding his own website to turn his brilliant idea into a functioning business.

Omidyar also generated buzz around his brand when his PR manager fabricated the story that eBay was created to find Pez Dispensers for the founder's wife. That story was picked up by media across the world, undoubtedly helping the site attract countless new users. I'm not condoning it, but talk about great low-cost marketing! The company soon caught the attention of venture capitalists, and before long, eBay had become a Fortune 500 company.

From free guerrilla marketing opportunities, like Facebook, Twitter, and YouTube, to free and low-cost business applications, such as online project management software, customer relationship management programs, email, and cloud telephony, there's an endless supply of resources available for bootstrapping your business.

You can also leverage the Internet to find low-cost labor resources, including freelancers, city and county work programs, and much more. Simply stated, technology makes it possible to do more with less than ever before.

## *Seek help from the SBA*

Starting your own business is the American Dream, and entrepreneurs play a major role in keeping our economy strong. Small businesses are truly the backbone of America. That's why, in 1953, the government founded the U.S. Small Business Administration (SBA). According to its website, the SBA "has delivered millions of loans, loan guarantees, contracts, counseling sessions and other forms of assistance to small businesses."

The SBA assists entrepreneurs in many different ways, including providing them with:

- Access to capital
- Government contracting opportunities
- Advocacy

Entrepreneurs can begin to take advantage of this resource by visiting the SBA's website at www.SBA.gov.

## Get enough money

A common mistake entrepreneurs make is to start their businesses without having enough money to really build it successfully. In a U.S. Bank study of reasons for small business failure, 79% of respondents cited "starting out with too little money" as a major cause of their collapse.

The reason for this is that many inexperienced entrepreneurs don't understand that they need to calculate their borrowing needs based on a worst-case scenario rather than their best-case, rose-tinted-glasses forecast.

So, whenever you're planning your business and considering your financial situation, you have to hope for the best but plan for the worst. Whether you're financing the startup yourself or raising capital from other sources, you must make sure you have enough money to support the business to success.

A primary focus should be cash flow. Without it, your dream will soon die on the vine when you run out of money after having tapped all the sources of capital that you could. Having cash flow from a business that is sustainable as soon as possible with sales of services or products is of paramount importance, not pursuing venture capital. You can't wait to get the perfect setup, the financial clock will be ticking and speed to market with a good strategy for your business is crucial. Do what you have to in order to get some cash flowing quickly and minimize any borrowing.

### *Get coaching from a professional business advisor*

Whether this is your first time starting a business or you're a serial entrepreneur, everyone can use a little help when it comes to financing a business. That's why working with a professional advisor can be a smart idea.

You could use someone by your side that can coach you and help you be successful in obtaining capital and getting some cash flowing. Remember, in this area, preparation is the key to success! With an outside business advisor, you'll have someone who brings an objective, unbiased point of view to the table and who can help you in important areas related to starting and growing a successful business.

Assistance of this nature can help in many ways, such as to gain important knowledge, create your business documents for success, analyze your industry, ensure your business strategy is sound and feasible, and identify opportunities for acquiring the capital your business needs to thrive.

An advisor also can help with the important follow through when it comes to things such as contracts and exit strategies.

Yes, hiring an advisor will cost you some money, but it's an investment that can pay off many times over when the advisor brings methods and templates to the table and helps you overcome the challenges, avoid mistakes, and increase your odds of success with acquiring capital and growing your business.

"Part of your heritage in this society is the opportunity to become financially independent."

~ Jim Rohn

# 7

## HOW TO OVERCOME BARRIER #4: LACK OF BUSINESS MANAGEMENT SKILLS

"If money is your hope for independence you will never have it. The only real security that a man will have in this world is a reserve of knowledge, experience, and ability."

~ Henry Ford

In many ways, running a business is like having a baby. First you have to go through the pains and joys of birthing. Yeah, that sounds like doing a start-up alright. Then both babies and businesses require constant care, attention, and love if you want them to grow to be healthy and strong. A baby requires food, bathing, constant health care, unconditional love, and around-the-clock attention. Likewise, a business requires marketing, employee management, customer acquisition, ongoing financial management, and an array of other tasks for nonstop care.

In other words, just having a great idea for a business isn't enough. Having a positive attitude and the will to be successful, while both important characteristics of the successful entrepreneur, are not enough either. To run a successful company, you must have business management skills. You must master the essentials of business management if you want to be successful.

A key word is execution. Lots of people have good ideas—in fact, entrepreneurs usually have lots of ideas—but the successful entrepreneur is one who can execute on the right good idea and deliver it as a successful launch and a self-sustaining money-making business. Don't get me wrong, ideas are important, very important. Without a good idea as the genesis and foundation you won't have the belief in your business that can sustain you in tough times, and neither will it be attractive to others to buy into it from a financing or purchasing perspective.

So given that you have the foundation of a great business idea, then it is about how entrepreneurial you can be in execution of the business. That means leading and coordinating, finding solutions to problems (read building bridges over barriers), being creative, innovative, and also, just plain old fashion sticking-to-it-ness and getting-it-done.

Of course, not all entrepreneurs have the training or experience to properly manage a business. In fact, 89 percent of company founders surveyed by Kauffman cited business management skills (more specifically, the lack thereof) as an important barrier to entrepreneurial success.

## Experience Matters

According to Swedish researchers Diamanto Politis and Jonas Gabrielsson in their paper entitled *Prior Career Experience and the Development of Entrepreneurial Knowledge*, "individuals with previous management experience are moreover generally found to have a higher likelihood of success" in their ventures. The authors go on to explain that prior business management experience leads to better business opportunities because entrepreneurs with management experience often have prior knowledge of markets, ways to serve markets, and of customer problems.

A case study published in *European Management Journal*, stated that "prior general management experience is arguably a strong predictor of entrepreneurial success." The authors go on to suggest that business school students who have ambitions of starting their own company are best advised to first get a "real job" with management responsibility so they can acquire management skills and build entrepreneurial success from this foundation.

Also, in *Psychological Dimensions of Organizational Behavior*, Barry M. Shaw suggests that entrepreneurs with vast business management experience are more capable of finding ways to starting new companies than those with different career paths.

Further supporting the case that prior management experience can be helpful in entrepreneurial endeavors, in the Kauffman study of company founders, 98 percent of those surveyed ranked prior work experience as an important success factor, with 58 percent ranking it as extremely important.

I can tell you that my experience as a principal and director in consulting firms in developing new methods and practices in new lines of business and also assisting clients in developing their businesses has helped me greatly with starting my own businesses. My experience and the lessons I've learned along the way have undoubtedly made me better prepared for all the challenges inherent with building a business.

In short, entrepreneurs with business management experience have developed the skills necessary for handling all types of situations and problems that arise when running a business. Those without prior management experience may not have the ability to handle all of the different aspects of managing a business.

But does this mean that people without an MBA or equivalent education and experience should not consider the entrepreneurial path? Absolutely not. I don't have an MBA, yet I've managed a lot of people with them and gave some of them a good performance review and others not. I've also had the privilege of managing and leading Naval Commanders, West Point Graduates, and so many other outstanding individuals as we successfully completed challenging business projects – but my educational experience was not the same as theirs. Vision and leadership qualities are not necessarily instilled into us just through education but also through experience and development of character.

I'm not advocating the abandonment of a proper education; in fact, I support it. But Bill Gates did not have an MBA or any kind of educational degree prior to his success. Ray Kroc, founder of McDonalds, dropped out of high school as did Sir Richard Branson, billionaire founder of all the Virgin Enterprises.

Entrepreneurship is an equal opportunity path, and in a free informational society, you have the ability to educate yourself and gain the skills and experience you need to be successful. There are ways to get the information you need to bridge the gaps and crossover to a better place of preparation for success.

**Essential Business Management Skills for Entrepreneurs**

Understanding what it takes to manage a business successfully is the first step to being a great leader. You have to know how to integrate your team and activities in a manner that allows you to achieve your company's goals efficiently and successfully.

Later in this book when discussing our new proprietary system to developing an entrepreneur and their business, we identify major domains of activity necessary to support the establishment and execution of carrying out the business. One of those domains we call out is management, and also discuss in a greater level of detail the subdomains within it as different types of entrepreneurial management needed. For now we will limit ourselves to looking at some business skills required of an entrepreneur to manage a business.

Which business management skills are most important for entrepreneurs to master? A lot goes into managing a business, but here are some of the skills I believe entrepreneurs need to develop to manage their businesses effectively.

**1. Sales and Marketing**

Marketing is of critical importance to the success of your venture. Marketing is everything that you do to get your product or service in front of your customers. Marketing goes into the development of your company, your capital-raising efforts, your recruiting, and of course, your sales.

Marketing has a lot of different facets, such as public relations, lead generation, networking, customer relationship management, pricing, packaging, partnerships, and distribution, to name just a handful.

Many entrepreneurs complain that it's just too difficult to generate buzz and make their companies stand out when they're competing with the big boys who have seemingly endless marketing budgets and earned name recognition. To that I say, build a bridge and get over it.

That's what this whole book is about—building bridges over challenges. Yes, it's difficult to market your business against the big boys, but successful entrepreneurs see opportunities where others see challenges. In many ways, you have an advantage over the huge corporations.

Don't believe me? Take a closer look. Here are just some of the marketing advantages you have over the big boys:

- **You can connect with customers on a more personal level**—While many corporations have jumped on the social media bandwagon to improve relationships with their customers, the reality is that small businesses have a huge advantage when it comes to creating personal relationships with customers. You can focus your efforts on giving your customers excellent personal service, taking the time to truly get to know them and understand their needs, and generating referrals from them.

- **You can throw out the rulebook and take advantage of creative guerilla marketing tactics**— Fitness First is a European fitness club. As a way to increase membership, they partnered with local restaurants to bring customers the "Calorie Receipt." At the end of the meal, the customer would receive a receipt that totaled up how many calories they just consumed. The receipt doubled as a voucher for a discounted gym membership. Or take a look at what Blendtec has been doing to promote their blenders. The Utah-based company has earned notoriety for its *Will It Blend?* series of viral marketing videos that are on YouTube, where the company founder blends different products, such as iPhones, glow sticks, iPads, marbles, Bic lighters, and more. These videos have earned hundreds of millions of views, helping the company get its product out to a huge audience in a creative, memorable, and cost-effective way. Talk about creative guerilla marketing! This is how you need to be thinking as an entrepreneur. Be daring. Break the rules to level the playing field.

- **You can act quickly to capitalize on opportunities**— You're the decision maker, so you can make things happen fast. At large corporations, it can take months before a marketing tactic passes through all the red tape and gets all the necessary approvals. You need to pay attention to the news and developing trends to create timely promotions that can bring you a lot of buzz and interest. For instance, when the GoDaddy CEO released a video of himself killing an African elephant, many people were outraged. Several of the smaller web hosting companies immediately launched promotions to accommodate disgruntled GoDaddy customers. HostPapa, a smaller web hosting company, pledged to make a $5 donation to Save the Elephants charity from every domain transfer from former GoDaddy customers.

- **You can play up the small business angle**—Small businesses are the backbone of this country, and many consumers would rather give their money to a local small business than to a massive corporation. Heck, there's now even the annual Small Business Saturday event from American Express that encourages consumers to show their support for local businesses on this day and throughout the entire year. Americans love entrepreneurs, and as a small business, you have the opportunity to capitalize on your size and your story to steal business away from the big boys.

- **You can snap up remnant ad space at pennies on the dollar**—How did Tim Ferris, author of *The Four Hour Work Week*, buy $250,000+ of radio advertising for just $10,000? He took advantage of remnant advertising. Remnant ad space is the ad space media companies are unable to sell. In Ferris' case, the ad space became available when a big pharma advertiser pulled out a week before the ads were supposed to hit the air. The station was desperate to find advertisers to fill the now empty space, so they held a fire sale on the ad space. This happens all the time. Remnant space can be found in magazines and newspapers, on billboards, on TV, on the radio, on websites…just about everywhere, and you can get it at huge discounts (sometimes 75% or more off regular prices) because the media companies would rather sell this leftover space cheap than not sell it at all. Now, this begs the obvious question, "How do you find remnant advertising opportunities?" There are two basic ways to go about it. If you know which publications you want to target, you can contact them to find out about their current advertising opportunities. You'll likely have to do some negotiating with them to get them down on their price, and not all entrepreneurs have time for this. Your other option is to use a remnant ad buying agency that specializes in negotiating discounted ad rates for clients. There are many of these agencies out there. Just be sure to do your homework and verify that an agency is reputable before you hire them to buy ad space on your behalf.

Of course, these are just a few of the many marketing advantages small business owners have over their corporate competitors. It all comes down to embracing your size and the flexibility it gives you. Always be looking for opportunities where others see challenges.

But as you already know, marketing is only one piece of the puzzle. The smartest marketing strategy in the world means nothing if it doesn't get sales. Marketing will get your name out there, get your product in front of your target audience, and even bring customers to your doorstep, but it won't close the sale. That's why you have to possess strong sales skills. You have to know how to close the deal, or else all those marketing dollars will go to waste.

To start boosting your sales skills, you should:

- **Be comfortable with what you're selling**—Knowing your product or service forwards and backwards is a key first step for selling. Knowledge and familiarity with your product will breed confidence, making you more effective at closing the deal.

- **Understand your target audience's buying habits**— Depending on the item you're selling, customers will have a very specific buying process they follow. For example, if the item you're selling is very expensive, you'll probably notice that customers take longer to make a decision. They'll spend more time researching the product, exploring similar products from your competition, negotiating with you, etc. On the other hand, if the price is too low, customers may suspect that the quality of your product is lacking. You need to study your target audience and understand how they think when it comes to making a purchase. This will help you sell to them more effectively.

- **Build relationships**—Establishing rapport with customers is an important step to earning their business. If customers don't know you, don't trust you, or don't like you, they're not going to do business with you. Get plenty of face time with your customers, so you can earn their trust and close the sale.

- **Nurture relationships by being present**—Once you've started to build trust with your customers, you have to stay on their radar. Being on the top of their mind is how you'll make sales and build a loyal customer base. You can accomplish this in many ways, such as sending a monthly email newsletter to customers, updating your blog regularly, interacting on social media, hosting events, and even picking up the phone to call your customers.

Remember, no one is going to be more invested in the success of your company than you are. That's why you should never remove yourself from sales and marketing. You know your product better than anyone else, and you have the most to lose if your company fails. Stay involved, and give customers that personal touch that only an owner can provide.

## 2. Managing Expenses

Make no mistake. If you can't manage your expenses properly, your business will fail. Healthy cash flow is essential to your business' success. And while mastering expenses is a huge challenge for the entrepreneur, it's a challenge that must be conquered.

How can you build a bridge over the imposing barrier of managing your expenses?

- **Prioritize your expenses**—Growing up as a country boy of modest means, I quickly learned the difference between needs and wants. It's a skill that I've been able to carry over with me into being a business owner. As a business owner, you're faced with all types of expenses, but not all of them are necessary. Separating the necessary expenses from the unnecessary ones is often the difference between running a profitable business and being the captain of a sinking ship.

- **Make cuts where you can**—Take time to examine all expense areas, no matter how small, to determine which things you can do without since these can really add up. You may need to trim some perks, like expensive company-paid cell phone plans for employees, in order to keep your expenses in line. Here are some areas you could look at to see if there is room to save on expenses: travel, staff, benefits, vendors, utilities, office supplies, and inventory.

- **Create a cash flow plan**—Projecting cash flow can help you be prepared for trouble before it hits you. While your cash flow plan won't be a crystal ball that magically predicts the future, it will give you an educated guess about knowing how much cash will be coming in and how much will be going out. Things to consider when preparing your cash flow projection include the amount of cash you currently have on hand, customers' payment histories, salaries and wages, rent, inventory, vendor fees, utilities, advertising expenses, other operational costs, sales projections, and more. Preparing a cash flow projection can be a daunting task, so you may want to consider hiring a business advisor to assist you.

- **Increase your receivables**—To have healthy cash flow, you need money coming in. That means making sales and getting paid in a timely fashion. The point is to improve the speed in which you make cash. There are several techniques you can utilize to increase your receivables, such as offering discounts to customers who pay their bills before due dates, requesting deposits on orders, performing credit checks on noncash customers, and sending invoices quickly.

- **Manage your payables carefully**—Sometimes, the amount of cash going out isn't the problem; it's the timing of the expense that cripples you. Managing your payables carefully can help you control your expenses with more precision. Some of the things you can do to manage your payables include making payments on their due date (rather than paying early and putting yourself in a cash flow bind), creating payment plans with vendors to spread out the costs of their services, taking advantage of discounts vendors may offer for early payments, and choosing vendors that have flexible payment terms.

## 3. Building a Team

Building a successful business usually requires more than just one person. It's often a task that requires a team that is committed to the success of your business.

Even if you're a solopreneur, you'll still likely need help from contractors and advisors to get your venture off the ground.

Your business team could include:

- Full-time employees
- Part-time employees
- Business partners
- Contractors
- Business advisors
- Vendors and suppliers
- Professional allies
- Friends
- Family
- Business and industry associations
- Customers

While your natural inclination might be to do as much as possible yourself, especially in the early days of starting your business, you're going to need to build a team to help grow your business and get it to the next level. You have too many tasks that will be pulling at your attention. You just can't do it all on your own. You need to focus on completing the tasks that are going to make you money, and you need to recruit the talent to handle all other tasks.

Of course, finding the right talent is the key to building a great team. Here are some tips to help you recruit the right people for your company:

- **Prioritize your hires**—There are many roles to be filled on your team, but you may not have the budget to acquire all the talent you desire right now. That's why you must decide which hires are essential and which can be put off until a future date.

- **Always be searching for talent**—You should always have your eyes and ears open for finding new talent, even when you're not hiring at the moment. Meeting talented people should be an ongoing task for every entrepreneur. That's why Paul English, the co-founder of travel website Kayak.com, asks recent hires to name the most talented people they know and then he makes an effort to meet them in less than one week.

- **Interview for chemistry**—Recruiting talent is about more than just finding people with the skills needed to carry out a task. Chemistry is essential to building a great team. You have to find people who share your values and click with you. You need people who are team players, so never hire an abrasive individual, no matter how skilled or intelligent they may be. And when you realize you've made a mistake in hiring, correct it and move on, not letting it take any more energy and time in remediation that is best used elsewhere.

- **Check the candidate's referrals**—I don't care how well you click with someone during an interview, you always need to perform your due diligence before making a hire. The truth is that some people interview really well and talk a great game, but when it comes time to perform, their skills simply aren't there. Take the time to talk to people from your candidate's former company to ensure they are as great as they claim to be.

- **Hire people who are smarter than you**—Robert Kiyosaki, author of the best-selling book *Rich Dad, Poor Dad*, says that "a good manager is one who hires people smarter than he is." Every person you hire should increase your company's intelligence level. Smart team members will get things done, propose new ideas, be attentive listeners, and create solutions so you don't have to micromanage them. In short, you want to hire fellow bridge builders.

- **Act quickly when you've found the right talent**—When you've found the right person for the job, you must be quick and decisive in hiring them. When I find a person good for my team I engage with them and stay engaged, such as by phone and email, until I have them onboard functioning on the team. English, the co-founder of Kayak.com, has a seven-day deadline for new hires. When he finds someone he wants on his team, he strives to get that person to accept an offer within seven days. Good talent with the right skills, experience and chemistry is a gem to find, and you don't want to lose a resource to competition due to inattentiveness and losing the connection.

- **Seek help from a professional consulting and staffing agency**—Not all entrepreneurs have the time, desire, or ability to find the right talent. Whether developing your staffing strategy, searching for talent, validating a candidate, finding a short-term contractor or a new key employee, a consulting and staffing company can help you achieve this. This helps you keep your eye more on the important aspects of your business.

## 4. Ability to Plan

The ability to plan is an essential skill for building the future of your company. It's a skill that you'll be required to use from the time you first start thinking about starting a business until the moment you're able to walk away and retire as a successful entrepreneur.

Planning comes into play early on in starting your business. Many business owners develop a formal business plan to create a path for the development of their business, but recent evidence indicates that creating a formal written plan may not be as essential to success as once thought. A study by Babson College analyzed 116 businesses started by alumni over an 18-year period. Comparing success measures, such as annual revenue, the study found no statistical difference in success rates between businesses started with a formal written business plan and those without them.

That's not meant to imply that you don't need to have a clear strategy for your business. There's a difference between knowing your business objectives and having a strategy for achieving them and completing the tedious task of filling out a formal business plan document. In other words, have a clear direction for your business, but you may not need to spend months slaving over the writing of your formal business plan. There are better uses for your time.

A good alternative to writing a formal business plan is to work with an independent business advisor. Bringing in a business expert with an unbiased opinion to review the feasibility of your business idea and to help create a clear strategy and direction for your company can be an efficient, effective way to get your business headed in the right direction.

But as I said earlier, planning is an ongoing task. From long-term planning for the future of your business to planning out daily tasks for yourself and your employees, you will always need to be planning to reach specific, measurable, timeline-driven goals. You'll have goals that may be days away and other goals that you want to achieve years down the road.

Here is a simple four-step plan that will help you plan better for achieving any objective:

- **Define success**—To ensure your plan guides you in the right direction, you have to define your goals. This may include creating short-term milestones that need to be reached on the way to achieving the bigger, long-term goals.

- **Develop your business strategy**— It's important to know the What, When, Where, Why, and How of your business. What I mean by that is you need to know how your business idea is going to actually become a feasible, profitable venture. I believe this is the most important step in helping you think through all the business areas necessary to gain success. Again, if you don't have all the knowledge and experience to do this correctly, find a good business advisor to facilitate you.

- **Create a work plan**—Again, you don't have to write out every detailed word of your plan. You just need to outline your goals, milestones, significant activities and write down other most pertinent details, such as which people will be involved, which tactics will be used, etc.

- **Track results**—After you have put your strategy through your work plan into motion, you need to track the results. Are you reaching the milestones you've set for yourself? If not, why not? Are the milestones simply not realistic? Or is your plan ineffective and in need of being tweaked? Collect data, review it regularly, and be flexible enough to adjust your strategy and work plan to help you reach your goals.

## 5. Communication

One of Apple CEO Steve Jobs' greatest skills was his ability to communicate. He was a masterful public speaker who inspired millions with his presentations. His public speaking style relied on storytelling, clear language, connecting the message to his audience, and eliciting an emotional response.

While not everyone is equipped to communicate as effectively as Steve Jobs, as an entrepreneur, you must be an effective communicator. Communication skills will help you succeed in nearly every facet of your business, from raising capital to networking to building great relationships with your employees to making sales, and everything in between.

Some of the various communication and relationship-building skills you should focus on developing include:

- **Making a lasting impression**—You want to be someone who people remember after they've met you. The best way to make a lasting impression is to make a strong first impression. As an entrepreneur, you're constantly networking. Whether you're meeting people by chance or by appointment, everyone you meet represents an opportunity. They could be a future client, partner, employee, vendor, or resource, so it's important to make a good first impression. Some of the ways to do this are to present yourself appropriately (look your best), be yourself (be comfortable with who you are), be confident, be positive, be engaging (small talk goes a long way to building strong connections), and be a good listener.

- **Public speaking**—The fear of public speaking is so common that it has been given its own technical name—glossophobia. Comedian Jerry Seinfeld once joked that because fear of public speaking often ranks as people's number one fear (even over death!), that "to the average person, if you go to a funeral, you're better off in the casket than doing the eulogy." According to *Forbes*, about 10 percent of people love public speaking; another 10 percent are genuinely terrified of it and get nausea and panic attacks when faced with speaking in public; and the other 80 percent get nervous but are able to fight their way through it. In other words, 90 percent of the population doesn't like speaking in public. But public speaking is an unavoidable part of being an entrepreneur. You have to give presentations to banks and possible investors, hold employee meetings, make sales pitches to possible clients, run information seminars, speak at networking meetings, etc. If you are a poor public speaker, you could hurt your brand's image. Fortunately, there are things you can do to reduce your fear of public speaking. Here are a few that help me:

- Get in some exercise, such as walking, an hour or two before your speech. This has personally helped me work off the jitters before giving a presentation.

- Take deep "belly" breaths to relax your body and slow your heart rate before and during your speech.

- Be prepared. I study the entire speech, but I don't focus on memorizing it word for word. I just want to make sure I know the key points. This will help you to be prepared, which will make you comfortable so you can do some ad-libbing while staying on message. This can make you seem more in command of the subject if done correctly.

- Engage and interact with the audience, so that you're speaking *with* them not *to* them. That can be the difference between keeping your audience interested and putting them to sleep. The interaction can also put the speaker more at ease.

- **Managing people**—Interpersonal skills are an invaluable asset for entrepreneurs. Having the ability to communicate effectively with your team will make you a better, more likeable boss. An entrepreneur with good interpersonal skills is able to manage people effectively without alienating them. Some of the things you can do to improve your interpersonal communication skills are:

  - Be a good listener

  - Be positive and happy

  - Show your team that you care about them and appreciate their hard work

  - Treat everyone with the same level of respect

  - Don't speak down to anyone

  - Be clear when giving instructions or outlining expectations for a task

  - Have empathy for others

- **Dealing with difficult people**—At some point in your entrepreneurial journey, you're going to have to deal with difficult people. Maybe you'll have an overly demanding client, or perhaps you'll have an employee who is difficult to work with. Knowing how to deal with difficult people smoothly is essential to the health of your business. Here are a few quick pointers that will help you deal with difficult individuals effectively:

- Separate the real issues from your emotions. Don't react emotionally; react pragmatically. Always take the high road.

- Use behavioral conditioning techniques to reward positive behaviors and ignore/punish negative, abusive behaviors.

- Confront the individual about their behavior directly in an appropriate, professional manner.

- If the behavior continues, remove the individual from your business life.

- If for some reason the individual cannot be removed or replaced, you simply must learn to deal with them. Let it go and move on as best as you can.

- **Being persuasive**—The art of persuasion is critical to entrepreneurial success. You must be persuasive when raising capital, making sales, and motivating employees. Simply stated, being persuasive helps you get the things you want faster. The good news is that being persuasive is a skill, and like any other skill, it's something you can learn and master. To be more persuasive, you must:

  - **Understand what motivates the person you're trying to persuade.** People are motivated either by what they stand to gain or what they fear losing.

- **Increase your perceived power.** Let's face it—people are more likely to listen to you if they think you're someone important rather than just some small-time businessperson.

- **Perform like a pro.** Brian Tracy said it best in an *Entrepreneur* magazine article, "a person who is highly respected for his or her ability to get results is far more persuasive and influential than a person who only does an average job." In other words, the better you are at what you do, the more persuasive you will be.

- **Treat others the way you want to be treated.** It's The Golden Rule, and it's essential for being persuasive. When you treat others with kindness and respect, they'll be more open to being persuaded by you in whatever you need.

## 6. Relationship Building

An entrepreneur's worth can often be measured in the quantity and quality of the relationships they have built. Your business' success will be built on a foundation of healthy relationships with customers, investors, employees, partners, vendors, and others who play key roles in positioning your company for growth.

It's like the old saying goes, "It's not what you know, it's who you know."

Through my years of building consulting business, I've made it a priority to build and nurture relationships with companies and individuals that were symbiotic to success. I've even built relationships with some companies that might technically be viewed as competitors, turning them into allies that help all of our businesses grow.

Of course, building relationships takes work. Whether it's with a customer, an employee, a finance company, or even a competitor, you can put these relationship-building strategies into practice to help your company thrive:

- **Communicate frequently**—Relationships can't be built without communication. You need to reach out to those you're trying to build relationships with on a regular basis. Frequent communication will help you get to know each other better, establish trust, and keep you top-of-mind.

- **Know how to listen**—If you've ever been married or in a serious relationship, you've probably been told, "You never listen to me!" When it comes to building relationships, listening is probably even more important than speaking. This goes for business relations too. You need to make the other person know that they're being heard. Listen to their needs, and find ways to address them. This will help you build rapport.

- **Get face time**—In this age of social media and email, face-to-face relationship building often gets overlooked. But in my estimation, it's still an important way to build strong, profitable relationships. Who are you likelier to remember and trust—the person who sent you a Tweet once or twice or the individual you shared a meaningful conversation with in person? You need to get face time as much as possible with the people you're building relationships with. There's just no substitute for that face-to-face, real life contact.

- **Provide value**—There is an economy to relationships whether personal or business. It requires being authentic and providing something of value to the other person so that they are also more willing to invest time, energy and things of value in the mutually beneficial relationship. There are so many elements of value one could provide as information, introductions and support at difficult times.

- **Give it time to grow**—Relationships don't come full grown. They take time and require constant nurturing. According to Ivan Misner of *Entrepreneur* magazine, as relationships grow "fed by mutual trust and shared benefits, they evolve through three phases: visibility, credibility, and profitability." The stronger a relationship grows with time, the more profitable it becomes. Make sure you give your relationships the time and attention they need to become fully realized.

## 7. Dealing with Criticism

Winston Churchill wisely noted that "the price of greatness is responsibility." If you want to be a successful business owner, you are going to have to step up and take responsibility, and when you do that, it often means standing in the line of fire to take criticism from all around.

Being an entrepreneur means taking criticism. You will probably face criticism from friends and family who think you have no chance of achieving your dreams, employees who think you're a bad boss, customers who just can't be satisfied, competitors who want to see your company fail, and media members who want to pick you apart.

There are a few things you need to know when it comes to dealing with criticism:

- You will never please everybody. Stick to your vision (provided it's valid and feasible), and don't let anyone bring you down.

- Assess the criticism honestly to determine whether or not it's valid. If you don't think it's based on facts, then ignore it, get fired up, and stay committed to your dream.

- If the criticism does have some validity, embrace it as an opportunity to learn and better yourself so you can be a more successful entrepreneur.

One thing I do want to point out is that it's dangerous to ignore criticism. Some people will boldly tell you to just ignore the critics and keep doing what you're doing.

Ignoring criticism could possibly set you up for failure. As marketing authority Seth Godin said, "more often [than not], that feedback you're getting represents the way a hundred or thousand other customers are judging you." In other words, most criticism you receive isn't just being fabricated out of thin air. It's usually representative of how a larger percentage of individuals perceive you or your company.

That's not meant to imply that all criticism is valid and worthy of acting upon. The point is that you always need to be aware of how others perceive you, and you need to take an honest look at the criticism to determine if it's merited. It may be presenting you an opportunity to improve your business products or services and thus improve the success of your business.

One way to get an honest assessment is to seek the counsel of an independent business coach. A business coach won't have any personal bias, so their coaching and mentoring could provide a straightforward analysis that will let you know whether or not the criticism is truly valid and if so, what you can do to address it.

## 8. Managing Your Time

Time management is one of the toughest things for an entrepreneur to master. As a business owner, your plate is overflowing with things you have to do. Your attention is constantly being pulled in a thousand different directions, your to-do list is always growing, and there are just never enough hours in the day for you to get things done.

Remember, the time and effort that it takes to be an entrepreneur is one of the biggest barriers to entrepreneurial success. I've already touched on some of the bridge-building solutions to this challenge in the Time and Effort chapter, but I'd like to offer a few more pointers to help you be more productive.

- **Plan time for interruptions**—You're going to get pulled away from what you're doing or trying to do at least several times a day. There will be fires to put out and new tasks that pop up. That's just the reality of being an entrepreneur. If your schedule is already fully booked, these interruptions will throw you off. By leaving a little extra time for the inevitable interruptions, you're likelier to be able to stay on track.

- **Document everything you do for a week**—Take a little notebook with you to record your activities for a week. I bet you'll be shocked at how much time is wasted on unproductive actions, conversations, and thoughts compared to how much time is used to actually grow your business and make you money.

- **Take breaks to prevent burnout**—Jack Dorsey, co-founder of Twitter, runs two companies worth over a billion dollars each, and he still takes off Saturdays to rest and prevent burnout. I don't care how busy you are, you have to find the time to rest. Believe me, there will always be work to do, but you can't work 24/7. We all have productivity limits, and when you try to exceed them, you become less effective.

- **Know when to say "no"**—Adelaide Lancaster, entrepreneur, author, and co-founder of In Good Company, shared with CBS News that "savvy entrepreneurs recognize that that not all opportunities are created equal. Many are merely distractions that drain the company of important resources, such as focus, energy and time. Others may even imperil the whole venture. Successful entrepreneurs cultivate their own restraint, saying no quickly and frequently in order to stay on track." Saying "no" to things that will waste your time is going to help you be more productive and less overworked.

## 9. Learning New Skills

The successful entrepreneur is a lifelong learner, and learning new skills to manage your business venture more effectively is essential to your ability to be successful. They are always learning new skills and strategies for building bridges over any barriers that impede their success.

You should always keep an open mind, and be prepared to listen and learn from everyone. You should be a voracious consumer of books, blogs, magazine articles, podcasts...anything that can help you learn something new that you can apply to improving your business.

Entrepreneurship education can manifest itself in many different forms, from schools to working with mentors to learning from your daily experiences.

To be a true lifelong learner, you must:

- Admit that you don't know everything.

- Schedule time each day to learn and get better.

- Surround yourself with smart people.

- Seek out other successful entrepreneurs and experienced business advisors

- Learn from your mistakes and those committed by other entrepreneurs

- Always be reading

The best way to sum it up is like this—the successful entrepreneur always seeks answers to questions they don't have the answers for. When they find someone else who has the answer, they are not too proud to prevent it from enhancing their education.

I cannot stress the importance of this point enough. You must always be learning. Even the world's most successful entrepreneurs—Branson, Cuban, etc.—are still learning new ways to make their businesses better.

Want to be a successful, bridge-building entrepreneur? Better have an insatiable appetite for knowledge.

## 10. Delegating

Theodore Roosevelt once said, "the best executive is the one who has sense enough to pick good men to do what he wants done, and self-restraint to keep from meddling with them while they do it."

Once you've hired or contracted the best talent for your team, it's time to start letting them do their jobs. Of course, your business is your baby, and it's only natural to be protective of it. But the best entrepreneurs understand that if they are going to build bridges over the various barriers that stand in the way of their success, they're going to have to let others pitch in to construct the bridge properly.

But many entrepreneurs find excuses not to delegate. They say they're too busy to take the time to train someone. They say they lack the time to properly explain projects. They claim they're the only person who can get the job done right.

And what happens? A lack of project management can lead to projects getting backed up, other important tasks getting overlooked, and those tasks that you do complete getting done in an insufficient manner, all while your employees go underutilized and unfulfilled.

This is where a project management focus for your important business efforts can be truly invaluable. In our PMO (acronym for Project Management Office) Consulting services company experience, we have found that when busy business owners first provide guidance and objectives, and then turn over to a PMO the strategy, planning, and execution management of their important business improvement initiatives, they realize more project success and greater business improvement and value.

This can be provided for in many flexible ways, from finding a PMO consulting service to be your PMO, to having a PMO consulting service help you implement your own PMO, or just providing staff and expertise to fill important gaps. You can find more information on this at www.pmoconsulting.com.

Delegating is essential to entrepreneurial success. Richard Branson, founder of the Virgin empire and billionaire, told *Entrepreneur* magazine that "Virgin's ability to grow and diversify successfully was set in the company's early days, with my learning how to delegate and let go."

Branson goes on to say, "when employees tell you about their good ideas for the business, don't limit your response to asking questions, taking notes and following up. If you can, ask those people to lead their projects and take responsibility for them. From those experiences, they will then have built the confidence to take on more and you can take a further step back."

Here are some basic tips that will help you delegate responsibility more effectively:

- **Identify the right person or company for the job**. Sometimes, this means choosing someone internally or externally who's passionate about the project, willing to listen and learn about the business, and can provide the knowledge and experience necessary to complete the task properly.

- **Outline the goals of the project and important steps that are involved.** The clearer the explanation of the task, the likelier it is that it will be completed properly.

- **Create milestones.** Make sure your employees or contractors understand when you want the project completed by and when certain milestones should be reached. This will give you a good way to monitor their progress.

- **Give them room to breathe.** If you've hired the best talent and assigned the task to the right employee, you can take a step back and let them get the job done. Give them some space to work. No one responds well to a micromanager.

## Sharpen Your Business Management Skills

Improving your business management skills is an ongoing task that requires constant education. I encourage you to constantly keep a lookout for sources that offer ongoing support for entrepreneurs by providing straight-forward, proven strategies for starting and growing your business. Consider signing up for our free eNewsletter, you'll also receive a free download of my CD "7 Secrets to Entrepreneur Business Success." Learn more today at www.successfulentrepreneuradvisor.com.

"Of all the things I have done, the most vital is coordinating the talents of those who work for us and pointing them towards a certain goal."

~ Walt Disney

# 8

## HOW TO OVERCOME BARRIER #5: LACK OF KNOWLEDGE HOW TO START A BUSINESS

"Set impossible challenges. Then catch up with them."

~ Sir Richard Branson

Having the desire to do something and doing it are two totally different things. When I was a kid, I wanted to be a jet fighter pilot. I had a plastic fighter jet I would walk through the house zooming around and landing and taking off with it. I wanted to fly at high speeds and do outstanding maneuvers. To actually do this, I needed to learn about aerodynamics and everything else that it takes to be a great fighter pilot, but I never did gain the knowledge to become one.

The same is the case for many aspiring entrepreneurs. There are lots of people out there who have the desire to leave the rat race and start their own business, but they don't have the knowledge to do it. You may be one of those people. You might want to be an entrepreneur, but you just don't know how to do it.

You are not alone. Of those company founders surveyed by Kauffman, 84 percent identified lack of knowledge about how to start a business as an important barrier to entrepreneurship. It was rated as one of the top factors that prevents others from becoming entrepreneurs and as one of the top causes of failure for those who do take the plunge and try to start a business.

Simply stated, if you want to start a business and be successful at it, you need to acquire the necessary knowledge of how to start a business and learn the specific skills necessary to be a successful entrepreneur. You need to have the knowledge necessary to develop a business idea, scrutinize it thoroughly, bring it to reality, and make it profitable and sustainable.

## Acquiring the Knowledge Necessary to Start a Business

If you don't know something, you must learn it. For aspiring entrepreneurs who don't know how to start a business, the first and most important task at hand is to acquire the knowledge necessary to do so.

But how does one go about doing this? Do you have to get back in school and get your MBA if you want to be a successful entrepreneur? Can you head down to your local book store and get a few of those books written for "dummies" and learn it that way? Can you draw on your past work experience? Or can you just attempt starting a business and get your lessons from the school of hard knocks?

There is a little something to be said for each of these educational methods; so before we start exploring some of the nitty-gritty details about starting a business, let's take a closer look at what you can do to bridge the knowledge gap and better prepare yourself for success.

- **University education**—Perhaps the most obvious path to acquiring the knowledge needed to start a business is to go to school. After all, 70 percent of those surveyed by Kauffman said their university education was important. In particular, those who attended Ivy League schools placed value on their university education, with 86 percent citing it as important. Furthermore, a previous Kauffman paper had documented that 95 percent of the company founders surveyed had earned Bachelor's degrees and 47 percent had more advanced degrees. According to the U.S. Census Bureau, a little more than half of all business owners in the United States have a college degree.

  But wait. What about Bill Gates, Michael Dell, Steve Jobs, Larry Ellison, Mark Zuckerberg, Ralph Lauren, Richard Branson, and David Geffen? These are just a handful of Fortune 500 CEOs that dropped out of high school or college and went on to become billionaires. They didn't have to get their fancy degrees to learn how to start a business. So, does college matter for success? Does getting your degree really prepare you for success? As the previously cited *Entrepreneur* magazine article wisely points out, even though only a little more than half of all business owners have a college degree, "business owners are fairly old on average…that means they graduated high school decades back—in an era where there were more opportunities workers could pursue without a four-year degree." In other words, many of these business owners were able to get by without a degree because college simply wasn't as important a few decades ago as it is today. Not having a college degree in this day and age can make it difficult for an aspiring entrepreneur to get that real world, 9-to-5, on-the-job experience that so often serves as a launching pad for starting a successful business. Furthermore, higher education offers better support for entrepreneurs today than it has in the past. More than 1,600 schools now have programs specifically designed to prepare budding entrepreneurs for success, and those numbers are continuing to grow. In fact, there has been a 533 percent growth in the number of schools offering courses and programs in entrepreneurship since the 1980s. Colleges also offer ample resources, such as mentors, peer help, networking opportunities with investors, business plan development assistance, and much more.

So, where do I come out on all of this? The fact is you don't need a degree to start a business and succeed. Simply having a degree isn't automatically going to make you a successful entrepreneur. There are many intangible qualities, such as creativity and determination, that simply cannot be taught in school. However, a good entrepreneurship program at a university can bring you a little closer to bridging the knowledge gap to starting a business. Although it can be slower and not as beneficial as an experiential and more accelerated approach. I encourage every young, aspiring entrepreneur to at least give college an honest shot. No, it's not for everyone and you won't learn everything you need to know to be a successful entrepreneur, but a good education can provide you with a foundation and pool of knowledge to draw on when it comes time to start your business.

- **Books and other readily available resources**—Many great books have been written about how to start a business. Hey, you're reading a book right now that's packed with information that will help you get your business up and running so you can succeed as an entrepreneur! I'm a consistent reader. Even after all these years as a consultant and an entrepreneur, I still read every single day. I'm always interested in learning more about the various aspects of running a business and making it profitable. My education never stops, and neither should yours. Being an entrepreneur means being a lifelong learner. You will never know it all, but you have to keep reading and keep learning more. And by the way, that means admitting that you don't know it all. That's a hard thing for a lot of entrepreneurs, but it's so very important. If you can't admit that you don't know everything, your mind will close and you won't gain the knowledge you need to start and grow a business. Like Dr. Seuss once said, "The more that you read, the more things you will know. The more that you learn, the more places you'll go."

So, what exactly should you be reading? While this book is a good start, if I humbly say so myself, I fully admit that it won't teach you every single thing that there is to know about starting a business. No single book will do that. In fact, that's why I've started the *Successful Entrepreneur Advisor* series of books, so I can further explore with you all of the various aspects that go into growing a successful business. But I'm certainly not the only author who has something great to offer to educate you on starting a business. There are lots of really great experts, authors, and websites on starting a business. However, do your own research when traveling your individual path to discover your knowledge on entrepreneurship and starting a business. You will find books, blogs, podcasts, videos, whitepapers, and a host of other sources that can contribute to your entrepreneurial education and help you build a bridge over the lack of knowledge barrier. Be a relentless consumer of information anywhere you can find it.

- **Prior industry experience**—When consulting with aspiring entrepreneurs, I always encourage them to take a hard look at their real world experience to help determine what knowledge and skills they already possess that will be useful in starting a business. For example, someone who has spent years working his or her way up at restaurants as a waiter, cook, and manager would probably have a better chance of opening a successful restaurant than someone who has never worked a day in the industry. Your professional experience can be a great educational tool for learning how to start and run a business. In fact, the Kauffman survey found that 96 percent of company founders rated prior work experience as an important success factor; 58 percent ranked it as extremely important. This is what we call "domain experience" or industry experience. It's difficult to have a true understanding of what it takes to run a successful business in a particular industry until you've actually worked in that industry, living and breathing it. Is it absolutely necessary for you to have domain experience? Not at all. However, it's certainly a bonus and it can shorten the learning curve tremendously. Having domain experience isn't just helpful for giving you knowledge on how to start a business within a particular niche; it is also useful for networking. If you've worked in an industry for an extended period of time, chances are that you've built some valuable relationships along the way. These relationships can be leveraged for building your team, partnering with the right vendors, attracting clients, raising capital, and a host of other purposes.

Now, some would argue that having too much experience in an industry can actually be detrimental. They say that it can keep you from thinking outside of the box, prevent you from challenging industry norms, or make you jaded about what can and can't be done. Is there validity to this argument? Perhaps in some cases. But if I was a betting man, I'd put my money on the entrepreneur with prior industry experience to succeed over the one with no experience almost every time.

- **School of hard knocks**—A sure way to learn what it takes to start a business is to actually do it. No matter how much time you spend in school or how many books you read, there are some things you won't learn until you actually start building your own business. As Sir Richard Branson, the successful entrepreneur of the Virgin Enterprises says, "Screw it, just do it." What that means is to get on with something you are convinced about and try it; and I have long been an advocate of the phrase that Nike made globally famous, "Just do it." In fact, this was also the mantra that I used with business teams in delivering accelerated business solutions for companies, meaning to discuss a strategy and plan then get on with execution. Don't get into "analysis paralysis." There are certain lessons that just can't be taught and there is a time to stop strategizing and to do; you have to learn them through your own unique experience. Let me cite the Kauffman study again if I may. In this survey, 88 percent of the 549 company founders interviewed said that learning from previous successes and 78 percent said that learning from previous failures played an important role in their present successes. Furthermore, 40 percent said that lessons from failures were "extremely important." There's a reason that the Harvard Business School's paper *Performance Persistence in Entrepreneurship* found that serial entrepreneurs are about 12 percent more likely to succeed than first-time entrepreneurs. There's just no substitute for actual entrepreneurial experience. The more experience you have at starting your own business, the better you'll understand what all it takes to get a successful business off the ground. You'll learn from your mistakes, have an easier time obtaining the resources you need to start a business, and have a better plan in place for bringing your business idea to life.

Now, let me make one thing clear right now. I'm not advocating that you skip school, throw away the books, and ignore your prior industry experience in favor of starting a business right now. That's not what I'm saying at all. What I'm encouraging you to do is to use those things to create a solid foundation of knowledge for yourself, but at a certain point, you have to just get out there starting your own business, take the plunge, and keep learning as you go. That's the real key—keep learning, never stop! I'm still learning today, and I've been in business for decades. I still make mistakes, but I try to learn from them and not make the same mistake twice. I also support my ongoing education through constant reading and studying to help me find new strategies for growing a business and avoiding other major mistakes.

So, as you can see, there are many ways you can acquire the knowledge you need to start a business. You just have to be willing to learn and willing to make some mistakes along the way.

Being an entrepreneur is a constant education, but if you're committed to learning and use all the tools available to you, you can succeed.

There is also a way to learn more about the experience, skills and methods of a successful entrepreneur which helps you avoid some of the hard knocks and increases your opportunities of success. A program where you can benefit from research, case studies and experience so to learn more quickly about entrepreneur competencies and methods.

## The Accelerated Entrepreneur™ Roadmap

Now that you have a better understanding of some of the ways you can acquire the knowledge you need to start a business, there are other questions you may have about this that need to be addressed. Do you know where to start? Do you know what opportunities are available to you? Do you know the steps you need to take to realize your success starting a business ? Or if you have already started a business, do you have methods available to improve your business?

Wouldn't it be great if there was a roadmap that provided the average person a rapid, systematic approach from learning the characteristics of an entrepreneur and discovering business ideas to starting your own business or improving it, guiding you along the way? Imagine an entrepreneur bridge taking you from the beginning in discovering and understanding your assets and opportunities to actually establishing your business and making your dream a reality. Like in the story *The Wonderful Wizard of Oz*, all the character Dorothy had to do was follow the yellow brick road to reach the Emerald City. There is such a roadmap. You can follow a yellow brick road to your Emerald City of potential entrepreneurial success.

**My experience with accelerated solutions for business**

While spanning two decades in consulting with businesses and individuals, I have focused on developing and implementing business enterprise organizational, process and technology solutions to transform businesses. Along the way, there was the realization that for companies to gain business success and increased value in as cost effective a manner as possible, there was a need to formulate accelerated implementation solutions to facilitate them. This was necessary as a way to help prevent failure of business initiatives, promoting success by rapidly implementing valid business opportunities at minimum cost.

My focus was to identify and create easy-to-follow solution roadmaps with the needed templates and guidance that enabled individuals and businesses to complete efforts in weeks instead of months, and months instead of years while reducing the failures and the cost.

From these experiences I had in developing and utilizing accelerated business solutions successfully, and from my entrepreneurial business research and experience, I realized there was the lack of such a structured rapid approach available for any individual to follow in their pursuit of success as an entrepreneur. As I reviewed entrepreneur case study after case study, I found there was a consistent pattern of aspiring entrepreneurs challenged by the lack of a path forward and many finding their way by accident, if they were lucky.

I saw the need for an approach that would provide average entrepreneurs with a better opportunity to successfully start or improve a business. If one hunted hard, read a lot of books, and actually had the opportunity to talk with and spend time with experts, even then you could only find pieces of it but not the entire mosaic of a structured accelerated approach to facilitating entrepreneur business success.

Not everyone has the opportunity to spend time in Silicon Valley or Alley, not everyone is able to read hundreds of expert books on various business subject matters, and not everyone has been fortunate to have significant experience in business and associated systems and methodologies. There was a need for a roadmap that the average person could follow if you want to be an entrepreneur, start a business and have a better opportunity of success at it...a roadmap that helps you acquire knowledge of how to start a business and of the specific skills necessary to be a successful entrepreneur...a roadmap that could provide you a way to develop a business idea, scrutinize it thoroughly, and bring it to reality.

**Entrepreneur roadmap for the average person**

So I have developed the Accelerated Entrepreneur™ Roadmap. It is a dynamic rapid business development approach designed to foster faster business implementation with opportunity for higher quality results. This entrepreneurial roadmap for business success is based on principles of human asset utilization (you are your greatest asset), idea creation, dynamic business model design, strategic customer focus, and speed to realization of the business with a higher probability of success. It defines and accelerates the entrepreneur and their business opportunity with the roadmap and Accelerated Entrepreneur Toolkit providing guides and templates, and it replaces helter-skelter, stop-n-go experiences and failures with a well-defined roadmap and process to follow in the Accelerated Entrepreneur System.

The Accelerated Entrepreneur Roadmap puts a major emphasis on entrepreneur evaluation and business exploration upfront, which I believe are the initial seeds of success or failure. Once you've completed these important foundational phases, the rest is about following the Accelerated Entrepreneur Roadmap with solid execution. I believe that having a roadmap and the ability to execute it are absolutely fundamental to providing greater opportunity for the average person to experience success in starting a business. Lots of people have business ideas, but few are able to execute them to realization. This roadmap makes it easier to develop ideas and execute.

This successful entrepreneur approach is something that I've fine-tuned based on my years of business experience as both an entrepreneur and a business advisor. It can be revolutionary if you're starting a business as a first-time entrepreneur or very enabling to an experienced entrepreneur—following this roadmap can help guide and accelerate you to business success.

**A New Phased Agile Approach**

Many of the traditional business development attitudes and approaches to starting a business have been piecemeal and have remained the same for years. This has inevitably been a cause of costly delays and errors resulting in business failures. This accelerated entrepreneur approach is a more radical approach to business development that is rapid and agile, providing leading business practices in techniques and templates. This gives the aspiring or improving entrepreneur a dynamic framework which within they can learn, explore, and evolve until reaching business success.

Every activity that must be accomplished to successfully start a business can appropriately be grouped into natural phases of work that build one upon the other until ultimately reaching a successful business launch. This is what the Accelerated Entrepreneur Roadmap provides. The system is a rapid business development approach where there are phases of the entrepreneur journey; there are signposts of progress as you continue along the roadmap; there are tollgates you pass through from one phase to the next one; there are items to be completed for each tollgate which the next phase will use and build upon-- all leading you up to reaching the goal of a successful business launch.

As I've said, I believe that becoming an entrepreneur and starting your own business is a journey. One that is always continuing as you learn and accomplish new things. With this roadmap you have a step-by-step guide that helps you do this. Essentially, the Accelerated Entrepreneur Roadmap is an entrepreneur rapid business development method (E-RBDM) that enables a more quality business to be identified and implemented faster, saving valuable time and resources and accelerating the connection to customers and cash.

Traditional business development has been more linear, that is, do planning, then designing, afterward the build-out, and then the launch. E-RBDM compresses this into a rapid iterative development from a solid foundational base. There are tremendous techniques in this roadmap system to develop or improve a business.

There are five steps or phases in the rapid business development approach of the Accelerated Entrepreneur Roadmap. They are built upon what I call the RtC concept. They are Rapid to Convey, Rapid to Create, Rapid to Confirm, Rapid to Connect, and Rapid to Cash. Each one of these accelerates you toward the goal of having a better opportunity of establishing a successful business and making money. Let's review what the five steps are and some of their elements.

## 1st Phase: Rapid to Convey

The Rapid to Convey phase communicates to the individual the importance of viewing themselves as a human asset and resource with great potential. It helps them to inventory their experiences and skills that can be leveraged in discovery of their opportunities. It also conveys the competencies of entrepreneurs discovered from many case studies to help the individual understand their strengths and weaknesses so they can improve themselves and their opportunity of success. Embarking on the entrepreneurial path is truly a journey of discovery where you will not only discover much about business but more importantly much about yourself.

Before you can start a business, you need to take a cold, hard look in the mirror. Do you have what it takes to be an entrepreneur? What skills, experience, knowledge and intangible qualities are you bringing to the table? What are your strengths, and more importantly what are your weaknesses?

There is already a chapter in this book devoted to discussing the characteristics of a successful entrepreneur, so I don't want to spend a lot of time rehashing that here. However, as I mentioned earlier, it's important to perform a thorough entrepreneur evaluation in the beginning, because if you don't, you could be setting yourself up for failure.

You need to ask yourself, "What makes me think I can be a successful entrepreneur? What do I have or know that can be used for business success? How do I compare to what has been learned about the competencies of successful entrepreneurs? How can I improve myself and my opportunities of success?"

Some of the areas you should look at when considering such questions:

- **Your experience and business knowledge**—In an Ernst & Young survey titled *Nature or Nurture? Decoding the DNA of the Entrepreneur*, more than 50 percent of the entrepreneurs surveyed described themselves as transitioned entrepreneurs—entrepreneurs who had prior on-the-job experience in their industry. They went on to say that this experience as an employee was the most important factor to their success. Take an honest look at your experience. Look at your job history. What industries do you have meaningful experience in? Which types of businesses have you worked for? And what have you learned from your experiences that would help you in launching a business? I'm a firm believer that you increase your chances of success when you stick to your experience. The further you go from your core experience, the bigger the learning curve, the more costly the mistakes, and the higher your chances are of failing.

Essentially, I'm asking you to take an inventory of yourself. But it's not just about your professional experience. There are other important areas that require an honest self-evaluation. What skills do you have? For example, are you financially savvy? Are you a good networker? Do you know how to manage employees? What about sales and marketing, can you sell your product? Believe it or not, you don't have to be a jack of all trades to be a successful entrepreneur. Yes, you will likely be wearing many hats in the early stages of launching your business, but that doesn't mean you have to do it all on your own. The best, most successful entrepreneurs understand that it's smart to stick to your strengths and bring in outside help to fill in the areas where you have weaknesses. Of course, this means being honest with yourself. It means admitting that you don't know everything and it means being willing to give up some control. If you can't do these things, you might not be ready for success as an entrepreneur.

In my Accelerated Entrepreneur System, aspiring entrepreneurs are facilitated to perform an assessment of themselves with methods and templates provided from the Toolkit. This helps them to discover and understand their strengths, weaknesses, and opportunities, plus the risks they have as well. This positions them to be better prepared to take advantage of their opportunities. It also reviews with them the competencies of entrepreneurs identified from many worldwide studies so that the individual can determine where they may have gaps so that they have the opportunity to adequately fill them in by acquiring skills, knowledge, and new experiences. I've found this to be a great tool that fosters strategic thinking by the individual. Such analysis is best performed when multiple parties are involved. Even if you're just starting a one-person business, you would be well advised to hire a mentor to help you with this. This is one way I assist entrepreneurs. Also, in my Accelerated Entrepreneur Lab I take aspiring entrepreneurs through sessions utilizing the system and toolkit to speed them on their way. You can contact me for assistance, if you wish, through my website at www.successfulentrepreneuradvisor.com or at www.acceleratedentrepreneur.com.

If hiring a mentor isn't in your budget at the moment, then I also have accelerated entrepreneur products from the system available for self-study. You can learn more about these products to help you also at www.AcceleratedEntrepreneur.com. By utilizing these guides and also leaning on trusted people within your circle (perhaps a close friend, spouse, or colleague...somebody who has knowledge of you, your industry, and your business), you should be able to accomplish some straightforward analysis to help with completing your entrepreneur evaluation and opportunity discovery. Also, you can combine the self-study with spot consulting from a mentor which could give you better results at lower cost.

- **Your willingness to learn**— Great entrepreneurs are lifelong learners. They love to read, study other businesses, talk to other entrepreneurs and successful businesspeople, get help from business advisors and mentors, and absorb information wherever else they can find it. You need to be like a sponge. You should always be trying to soak up more information so that you can have a true competitive advantage. Knowledge truly is power. I've created the *Successful Entrepreneur Advisor* series for such a person. This series of books is for the entrepreneur who never wants to stop learning. It's for the entrepreneur who wants to push harder, learn more than all his competitors, and put that knowledge to use to build a more profitable business. An article in *Business Insider* sums it up best with its simple headline, "The Most Successful People Never Stop Learning until They Die." The article goes on to say that successful entrepreneurs should set aside time each day for research and education, interacting with expert peers and advisors who have knowledge you can absorb, being proactive in creating business ideas and following through on them, and having mentors they actually use and listen to, using their knowledge to add value to their business. I'll say it again. Loud and clear this time: NEVER STOP LEARNING! This will differentiate you from most of the crowd out there and provide you better opportunity.

- **Your willpower**—Being an entrepreneur is not for the faint of heart. You will have failures. You will make mistakes. Many of them, most likely. But what determines how successful you'll be is your willpower. Do you have the will to succeed? Are you persistent enough to get back up each time you fall down? History is filled with entrepreneurs who have overcome their failures to build successful companies.

Look at Bill Gates. When he was in high school in the 1970s, he and friend Paul Allen started the company Traf-O-Data, a computer business that automatically read paper tapes from traffic counters for local governments, according to *Entrepreneur* magazine. The idea soon became obsolete when the state of Washington started doing this for cities for free. Did Gates give up? No. Instead, he went on to create Microsoft and become one of the richest people in the world (in 2012, *Forbes* ranked Gates as the second richest person in the world with a net worth of $61 billion). Gates once said, "Success is a lousy teacher. It seduces smart people into thinking they can't lose." That's the attitude you need to have if you want to be a successful entrepreneur. With that level of willpower and that kind of positive attitude, you truly can build a bridge over any barrier that gets in your way.

- **Your intangible strengths**—There are certain intangible qualities that successful entrepreneurs possess that help them achieve greatness. I've mentioned that a closer look at the responses from successful entrepreneurs in both the Ernst & Young and Kauffman studies finds that some of the most commonly cited intangible characteristics of entrepreneurs include:

  o Creativity

  o Innovation

  o Passion

  o Faith

  o Optimism

  o Timing

  Some of the other intangible characteristics that I've witnessed in successful business owners over the years include self-confidence, courage, integrity, judgment, and the ability to work well with others.

When you're trying to identify your intangible traits, it's natural to be subjective and biased. The best ways to avoid this are to focus on concrete examples of instances in which you displayed a particular intangible trait and to get feedback from people who know you.

Do not skip this phase and its steps or try to rush through your self-analysis so you can hurry up and start a business. Evaluating yourself as an entrepreneur will lay the groundwork for your venture. It is the basis for important elements of your entrepreneurial journey that the next phases will use and build upon. Do it right, and you can find the appropriate opportunity for your unique skills, knowledge, experience, and personality. Do a halfhearted analysis, and you could be sowing the seeds of failure. It may be a good idea to utilize an experienced business coach certified by us in the Accelerated Entrepreneur System that can help with a proper evaluation that lays the right foundation.

Also, if you discover that the entrepreneurial path and starting your own business is not for you—it's ok. Understanding that now is important, preventing you from misdirecting your talents and resources. You can better focus on a career path that is best for you. However, don't cut yourself short and not take advantage of an opportunity to follow a proven roadmap to grow in a way you had never before dreamed possible and achieve great success with its benefits.

## 2nd Phase: Rapid to Create

The Rapid to Create phase provides a way for the individual to take the evaluation and discovery from the 1st phase and use it as input to assist with business idea creation, and then exploring the ideas that are specific to your profile that you could possibly support to business success. Also, it offers assistance with taking those ideas and expanding on them with concept visioning that leads into actual identification of business opportunities with their main high-level components. Finally, this phase involves initial screening and selection of those business opportunities that you believe have potential and want to carry forward for proof of concept.

So now that you've performed a thorough entrepreneur evaluation, time to start developing ideas for your business. Remember, you've identified your strengths, weaknesses, opportunities, and threats (risks), as well as your skills, experience, and knowledge; now, you need to use all of this information to guide your business idea creation.

During this phase of the Accelerated Entrepreneur Roadmap, your job will be to come up with business ideas and separate the good ideas from the bad ones.

Following are some of the considerations in doing this.

## Start Brainstorming

Don't just sit back and hope a good business idea suddenly comes to you as you're going about your day. While it could happen this way, the smart approach is to be proactive in your pursuit of the big idea.

Get out a sheet of paper, bust out the whiteboard, and/or sit around with colleagues and let the brainstorming begin. At this point, I want you to think of a funnel. You want to pour as much thought and ideas into it as possible. This is the time for "ideas gone wild." Don't be critical or rejecting at this point and not to worry about qualifying them now – just capture them. Think of "what if" and also "imagine for a moment" kind of ideas. Allow your passions and strengths to drive toward moments of inspiration where innovation and uniqueness can be born.

Imagine as many ideas as possible. Usually it will take looking at many ideas to get one business that can be successfully launched. Remember, your brainstorming sessions should be "naturally" guided by the evaluation analysis you performed earlier.

In the Accelerated Entrepreneur Toolkit there are several business brainstorming methods and other techniques available to facilitate your idea generation. Here is an example where you can find good ideas; as the previously-cited Harvard Business School study pointed out, most entrepreneurs draw from their work experiences at former employers in the generation of business ideas. The Harvard paper cites a 2000 study by Bhide that says that a substantial percentage of the Inc. 500 came up with their idea for a new company while working at their prior employer.

Think about your daily experiences you had as an employee. What are some of the things that frustrated you, that you knew you could make better? What are some of the complaints and pain points that customers seemed to share that your former employers weren't addressing? What were some of the opportunities that your former employers were overlooking or intentionally ignoring?

Because you have prior experience in an industry, you will be better equipped to separate the good ideas from the bad ones, because you have experienced hands in the field and you know what could work and what won't.


## Make sure your ideas won't get you in trouble

Now, I just want to note something briefly. Leaving your employer to start a business that might be competing with them could become a tough situation. There are legal factors that need to be considered and ethical factors as well.

Here are a few quick tips to help you leave the nest with as little fallout as possible:

- Review any contracts and non-compete agreements to make sure starting your new business won't get you sued.

- Consult with an attorney to make sure everything is on the up and up and you're clear to start your business.

- Don't burn bridges and try to hurt your former company by stealing clients, sharing trade secrets, or luring employees away.

- Be appropriate with your former employer in your dealings. Find a way that you can comfortably and profitably operate in your niche.

### Screen your ideas to find the business opportunities

After generating business ideas from the brainstorming techniques, you can start exploring and analyzing your ideas by expanding on them with business concept visioning so that the ideas can be screened. This business concept visioning approach from the toolkit assists you in doing several important things in this phase:

- **Defining your entrepreneurial vision—** Before you can arrive you must clearly see where you're going! Defining the business strategic intentions for yourself as an entrepreneur will provide you a clear vision of where you want to go in business. Accomplish this by defining the scope and boundaries of your business goals and the guiding principles for achieving those goals. This will provide you with the correct expectations that the right business concept must align with so to be chosen.

- **Defining the business concepts—** The Danish tale of the ugly duckling becoming a beautiful swan is one of transformation for the better. To know if a business idea has the opportunity to be something more, its business concept must be more fully described to see how attractive it can become. This is done by answering important questions such as what will the business do? Who are the customers? What needs of the customers are met by what the business will do? What is unique, different and valuable? How will this be achieved? What is the value proposition? The answers are input to fleshing out the business concept proposition, which is like a mini-business case with high-level components, so it's possible to know how attractive and feasible the idea may be.

- **Measure and score the business idea propositions—** Look for the best match of the business propositions to the entrepreneur. This is done by measuring the ideas and valuing how well the business concept aligns with your capabilities and interests and will ensure the best use and return on your talents, skills and resources. Scoring and rating the business ideas according to their attractiveness, feasibility and your passion will identify your best business opportunities.

The Accelerated Entrepreneur Roadmap with its Toolkit provides the methods and templates in this systematic accelerated process to facilitate visioning of you and your concepts you come up with so to assist you in expanding the ideas enough that you will be able to identify, screen, and select your business opportunities. Now you could have that big idea which you believe has the potential necessary to carry forward for proof of concept.

Of course, there is such a thing as being too close to your ideas and your passion. That's where it's helpful to get insight from an independent, unbiased source. An experienced business coach certified in the Accelerated Entrepreneur Roadmap system would be able to help with all aspects of idea development, from brainstorming to analysis to selection.

A word of caution, while you're still in the process of coming up with ideas for your business, you might be tempted to talk to friends, co-workers, or others about your ideas, but be careful. If you don't take measures to protect your ideas, someone (even someone you may think you can trust) could take your ideas and start their own business. Be smart and guard your ideas. A great idea is an invaluable asset.

## 3rd Phase: Rapid to Confirm

You think you've found the winning idea. Now is where some additional truly important work begins. Before you get ahead of yourself and try to launch your business, you have to restrain yourself a bit and actually confirm that the concept is feasible. This is the part of the Accelerated Entrepreneur Roadmap that I refer to as Rapid to Confirm.

This phase is designed for iterative business prototyping to evolve and test your business concept proposition from the previous phase. As you take it to a deeper level of detail and planning through an agile proof of concept cycle which enables you to rework and fine-tune the business model. It will lead you to either validating the business concept or to abandoning it as not viable. This phase is crucial to saving money, time and preventing business failures. Without yet having to make a huge commitment of finance and effort, you can have confirmed your belief in the actuality of potential commercialization of your business idea.

This is a step-by-step iterative process that, when completed, should clearly spell out to you whether or not you think your idea will work as an actual business. In the event that you find the idea isn't feasible, don't ignore the results, no matter how much it dismays you. Being too married to a single idea has been the downfall of many an entrepreneur. Instead, pivot to the next business opportunity and put it through this step-by-step analysis again.

In the effort to prove the validity of your business concept, here are some examples of the components of the process:

- **Visualize and define the business strategy and model**—How is your idea going to translate into an actual business? It's important to know the What, When, Where, Why, and How of your business blueprint. What I mean by that is you need to know how your business idea is going to actually become a feasible, profitable venture. Here you take the business concept proposition and define it in more detail with your business strategy and business model which is essentially about answering the question, "How are you going to make money?" That means you need to identify a number of key things that go into this such as:

  o **Your target audience**—Who exactly are you trying to reach with your product or service? Don't be general; get as specific as you possibly can. The more detailed you are with defining your target customers, the better prepared you will be to reach them and sell to them. When defining your target audience, look at things like their gender, income level, location, lifestyle, profession, interests, and buying habits. You should also look to see who your competitors are targeting. You aren't doing this so you can mimic them. Instead, you should be looking at how you can do it uniquely and better or for a niche market that they are overlooking.

o **The benefits of your product or service**—Why would anyone want your product or service? What problems does it solve? What challenges does it help them overcome? In short, how will using your product or service make your customers lives better? Your customers aren't just buying a product; they are buying a solution to a problem they're facing. You must do a good job of answering the "what's in it for me?" question that all customers will have, and the way you do this is by focusing on what problems your product or service solves. For example, Weight Watchers sells a service that helps you lose weight, but what they are really selling is a product that helps increase your confidence and improve your health. Monster Energy sells heavily-caffeinated drinks, but what they're really selling is a way for you to stay energized and alert after a long night out on the town or during a boring, never-ending afternoon at work. This is the mindset you need to be in when searching for the key benefits of your product or service.

o **Your unique selling proposition**—What makes you different than every other company you're competing with? If you can't answer this simple question effectively, you're going to have a hard time winning customers. After all, if your company and products are essentially the same as everything else that's already on the market, why would anyone choose to do business with you? Identifying your unique selling proposition (USP) is an important step to developing your business model. To do this, you should create a list of the features and benefits of your product or service, identify what need it's meeting, determine which characteristics of your product make it different than your competitors' products, and select the most compelling and meaningful differences you've defined.

- **Your sales and marketing strategy**—How do you plan to reach, acquire, and keep customers? Without customers, your business fails, no matter how great your product might be. You must have a clear strategy in place for getting your product or service sold and keeping your customers happy and loyal. If you aren't a marketer, either hire employees with a strong marketing background, turn to a marketing agency, or seek help from a business advisor. If you can't get your product marketed effectively, your company will fail.

- **Your strategy for generating revenue**—Where is your money going to be coming from? Who is paying you? How much are they paying you? How will they be paying you? How often will they be paying you? When focusing on your revenue stream, it's important to not just define how you expect to make money, but you also must define when you expect the money to come in. If you have high upfront costs and it takes too long before a revenue stream begins to flow, you can fail before you really have a chance to get started.

- **Your cost structure**—Now that you know where you'll be getting your money from, it's important to identify where your money will be going. You need to know all of your costs. This means identifying all of the upfront costs you'll have when starting your business, the ongoing costs of keeping your business up and running, and the source of funds that will pay for all of this. Again, you aren't just identifying what your costs will be; you are also identifying when these costs will hit. In other words, you're answering the who, what, when, where, why, and how questions of your cost structure.

o **Your profit margin**—At the end of the day, a business' success is about its ability to produce more revenue than it has costs. You need to have more money rolling in than is rolling out. So, once you've identified all your sources of revenue and all your expenses, you can calculate your profit margin. Will you be turning a profit? At what point do you project you will start turning a profit? How much of a profit will you be turning? While these are only projections, it will be helpful for seeing how realistic your business idea really is.

These are examples of the type of elements needing definition so to be used as inputs for the business strategy and model. There are many different business models out there. Some are tried and true; others are new and innovative. Some companies use a fusion of various business models to create their own unique one. The Accelerated Entrepreneur Roadmap is a system that recognizes the importance of defining the strategy and model for your business and provides a toolkit with templates and guidance facilitating you to accomplish this.

• **Build the business case**—The point of a business case is to provide all the information necessary to justify the resources and investment necessary to bring a business to fruition. Your business case needs to detail all the relevant and financial facts in all areas of your business model.

This technique will develop a clear understanding of the payback for the investment you will be making as it accumulates and processes critical information to determine the potential commercialization of the business, and it can also be used to support gaining financing of the business if that is involved. Your basic job is to capture all of the knowledge you've developed about how your business will run, and its costs, revenues and profit. You want to create a communication tool that gives you the information you need to objectively review the facts and assumptions about your business idea to determine if you should act on it or not. When developing your business case, consider these points:

o **Create a clear and compelling story**: Financial numbers, while very important, will not speak for themselves. You need to add value and intrigue to the numbers by supporting them with a compelling narrative.

o **Use fact-driven analysis:** Business decisions aren't based on opinions but rather on facts. You must use accurate, relevant information that reflects reality; measuring by both quantitative (quantity) and qualitative (quality) evidence. Trust the numbers.

o **Analyze costs and benefits**: It's extremely important to make sure you always ask the right questions, use solid evaluation, and ensure that assumptions are valid. Before making any expenditure, you must ensure that the benefits justify the costs.

o **Be open-minded**: It's not always easy, but if you want to be successful, you have to be objective and willing to listen and learn. Face the facts; don't shoot down the messengers.

If you've ever watched the hit TV show *Shark Tank*, you should have some understanding of the difference between a good business case and a bad business case. On this show, entrepreneurs pitch their business ideas to potential investors, trying to convince these successful business people to put their money on the line and buy into their business idea. Essentially, that's what you're doing with your business case. You're trying to make an argument that your business idea is one worth investing in.

- **Business testing with structured walkthroughs—** Structured walkthroughs of your business blueprint is a method to prototype and test it that will help you identify problems early on before you have committed significant investments of time and money and while it's still easier to adjust your business approach and expectations. This business modeling process projects you forward, transporting you through your business and reviews it in an analytical manner. It helps you identify errors in business design and assumptions that could go undetected until a later date when they would be more costly. This technique is not used as much as one would think and certainly not as much as it should. With this method, you can review and refine the business definition as tightly and effectively as possible at the time. There are various techniques in the Accelerated Entrepreneur Toolkit to support this business analysis such as:

  o **Business milestone charting**: A means of identifying and mapping significant business activities in the business cycle and confirming the critical path to success.

  o **Dress rehearsal business simulation**: A technique for traveling through a day, week, month, and year in the life of the business.

o **Business scenario modeling**: A method to identify and assess potential business scenarios.

o **Test cases**: An approach to developing scripts for testing the validity of the business scenarios.

o **Business value outlining:** A method of determining the sequence of inputs, the significant transforming business activities, and the resulting outputs to determine business value.

Essentially, with this approach and techniques you're reviewing your to-be business model. It can be an effective way to promote discussion, identify possible ambiguities or errors with your business model assumptions, and get everything nailed down. Helping you to review and refine until gaining confidence in the feasibility of the business to a point your comfortable moving farther ahead with it.

- **Prototype Market Probing**—This is another method of business validation that can be undertaken to see how the market might react to your business concept once it's launched. It is a customer-centric approach to further validate the business concept. Market probing is where potential markets are tested with simplified early concepts and versions of your products or services so you can gain market response test results and gauge consumer interest in your business. The point is to learn from these probes and use them to help determine the viability of your idea and to guide your future business development. If sample tests confirm market interest in your product or service, then you could be on the right track; whereas lack of response could indicate the business concept is invalid or in need of refining. Prototype market probing is a technique which requires some upfront research so that test results are of quality and impact. Depending on the business product or service, areas to consider doing prior research in could be industry, product, or service markets, competition, sales channels, consumer behavior and attitudes, advertising, and events. Such research will help position the market testing so that true and reliable first-hand market information is gathered in relationship to the business concept. There are various probing methods that can be utilized, such as interviews, surveys, websites, focus groups and others, based on what is viewed as having the greatest strength of results to help in decision making. Essentially, the market probing of the business concept serves as a vehicle for learning about the business and its potential reception, and very importantly, if whether and how it can be scaled up. With this approach, an entrepreneur may very well find the business concept confirmed or that their original business idea is lacking. But also, serendipity (meaning a happy accident or pleasant surprise) could also hand you an insight when using this method that is even more valuable than your initial concept.

- **Review, Challenge, Refine**—All during this phase while using the various methods, an entrepreneur is attempting to evolve and confirm their business concept. While doing so there is an important attitude to keep at the forefront. That is to put good faith effort into reviewing the business model and most importantly challenging it every step of the way. Looking for the opportunities to refine it with improvements and to eliminate errors and bad assumptions. At this stage of the roadmap process, you have enough information on your hands that you have a good idea of what's working with your business model, what can be working better, and what needs to be reworked. It's your time to do some tweaking and polishing of your idea.

If you identified any areas of concern when analyzing your idea's commercialization potential, you need to address them now. Find ways to refine and re-imagine your business model to make it the best it can be. This is where you're putting the final touches on everything to determine if you have a winning idea and to prevent failure and promote success, so leave no stone unturned.

- **Validate commercialization potential**—You've assessed the opportunity thoroughly with appropriate methods and techniques. Now you update and refine the business case with all of the information you've developed, tested, and refined. You're in a better place to confirm your belief in the business viability of your idea. So now it is time for the moment of truth: Can your idea be a profitable business? This isn't the place for emotions. You can't try to force the pieces to fit if they don't want to, and you certainly shouldn't ignore the facts of your findings. Do they confirm that the business concept will meet the expectations of your entrepreneurial vision and business concept proposition? If in your gut you know that your business idea is validated through this process, you're ready to move on to the next phase of the Accelerated Entrepreneur Roadmap and make the investments necessary to scale up and establish the business.

- **The Pivot**—However, if you've found that your idea just isn't a feasible business, you can pivot to another business idea you had explored in the previous phase; or as you worked to evolve and confirm your original business concept in this phase of the roadmap, you may have discovered an insight that is an opportunity (remember, being an entrepreneur is truly a journey of discovery). Perhaps it is only a few degrees variation of your original concept or a new cranial lightning bolt altogether. If you pivot, you can now filter the different business concept through the agile iterative process of this phase to rapidly confirm if you believe it is a viable business to commercialize.

This phase is designed as an iterative process of business defining, testing, probing, learning, refining and validating, or if necessary, pivoting to the next thing, until you find and validate a viable business idea. It will facilitate the entrepreneur to evolve his business ideas until he finds a path he believes in that will lead to commercialization and profit.

It does this without a full scale commitment of finance and other resources, all the while providing greater opportunity for ultimate success. It is essential to look at many ideas to identify one or two businesses that can be successfully launched and sustained.

A necessary ingredient for success in this phase is the entrepreneur characteristic of staying power to persist and learn through the surprises and hard work. But in the end, completing this phase of the roadmap better positions you for a real payoff.

## 4th Phase: Rapid to Connect

So you have that business strategy and model you believe in as your valid opportunity and are convinced to commit your resources necessary to make it a success. After confirming a business opportunity's viability, the next step in the Accelerated Entrepreneur Roadmap is to rapidly establish your actual business and connecting to the marketplace. This is the Rapid to Connect phase.

In this phase, guided by your previously developed business case, strategy and model, you will begin to bring the business from the lab to the market by establishing the foundation of your business in the major domains (key areas or disciplines of knowledge and activity) necessary to support the execution of carrying out the business. This sets you up so you can launch your business and maintain it as a profitable enterprise. This phase is designed to provide you guidance and information in the major business building blocks so that you can more quickly navigate this phase of building a business by focusing on the big picture important areas and not get bogged down by the multitude of little details that can divert your focus.

Major domains in the accelerated system drives you to focus on areas as legal, finance, team, technology, market, and management, all providing guidance to assist you in rapidly establishing the business. Furthermore, each of these primary business areas has significant sub-domains that the entrepreneur will need to focus on for their business success. The following areas are examples for this phase of the roadmap.

## Legal

There are many different legal issues to consider when it comes to starting your business. This includes from choosing a legal structure for your business to taking the necessary steps to protect your intellectual property, and much more.

The smartest thing you can do is to consult with an attorney and a seasoned business advisor who could provide guidance to you through the various legal aspects that need to be addressed when building your business and help ensure your legal ducks are in a row. Here are some examples to consider:

- **Choosing the legal structure of your business—** Choosing the legal structure of your business means identifying what type of business entity you are. Typically, a business can be either a sole proprietorship, partnership, corporation, or LLC (limited liability company). Choosing the right legal structure for your business is a detailed process, and I'm not going to attempt to fully tackle such a big subject in the confines of this book. However, I will quickly provide some definition of different business entities to help you better understand your options:

  o **Sole proprietorship—**With a sole proprietorship, you're the owner, and you are personally liable for all financial obligations to the business. It's the most simple, straightforward business structure, and it's common among many solo entrepreneurs.

  o **Partnership—**A partnership means two or more people share ownership in the business. Each partner shares in the profits and losses of the business, and each is personally liable for the financial obligations to the company.

  o **Corporation—**What makes a corporation different is that it becomes a separate entity from the people who founded it. The corporation is taxed and held legally liable for its actions, as if it was a person. This allows the individuals who start the company to avoid personal liability to the business, but it's more complex and expensive to form and run a corporation.

o **LLC**—An LLC, or limited liability company, is popular among many entrepreneurs because it combines the benefits of the corporation and partnership business entities. Owners share in the profits and losses of the business without the company itself being taxed, but they don't have personal liability. It's a good way to protect your personal assets while maintaining ownership and control of your company.

- **Choosing a name for your business**—Clearly, a business name is important. But there are many different schools of thought when it comes to choosing a name for a business. Some argue that it's best to choose an abstract name that you can define in any way you choose; others think a name should be clear and informative so customers know exactly what you do as soon as they hear your name. My thoughts? Choose a name that's catchy, appealing to your customers, fits your company's personality, is short and clear, and doesn't rely on a cute pun or inside joke. And of course, get your trade marking in place once you've found the right name.

You can consider taking advantage of some of the online services that are now available for taking care of the various legal aspects of your business, such as completing the documentation necessary for forming the legal structure of your business, getting a trademark for your business, etc.. Currently, LegalZoom.com is one example of such a service for creating and filing legal documents.

## Finance

Business and finance go hand in hand. It takes money to get your business off the ground, to keep it running, to keep your employees paid, to develop your products, and so on and so forth. Developing a sound financial foundation for your business will set you up for long-term success.

Some examples of financial issues that you will need to address during this phase of the Roadmap include:

- **Fundraising**—To state the obvious, it takes money to get a business up and running and to keep it operating on a daily basis. An entire chapter of this book is devoted to the topic of raising capital, so I suggest you refer to that portion of the book as this is a major barrier for many entrepreneurs. Remember, there are many different approaches you can take to financing your business, from using your own savings to seeking venture capital. When one door closes on you, don't get discouraged. Instead, pursue another avenue to get the financing you need to launch your big idea. Also, previous work you've done in this roadmap such as building out your business case will provide you with the information you need to support this.

- **Accounting**—You can easily get caught up in all of the fun and glamorous aspects of starting a business, but without a solid grasp of the numbers, your business simply will not thrive or survive. In fact, a Small Business Administration study entitled "Financial Difficulties of Small Business and Reasons for Their Failure" found that more than 28 percent of businesses declaring bankruptcy cite problems with the financial structure of the company as their main cause of failure.

Take a cue from this and make sure you learn the fundamentals of accounting. If you need to get help from an accounting expert, do so. Just make sure you don't overlook this crucial aspect of your business.

As an entrepreneur, you must be heavily involved in the financial side of your business. You must have a clear picture of your financial situation at all times. This isn't a task you can ignore or completely hand over to someone else. Stay in the know at all times.

## Your Team

Even if you're a solopreneur, you're going to be working with others in some form or fashion, whether it's with a freelancer who helps with your marketing or a business advisor who helps you with setting up your company for success. Having the right team in place can prove to be a key for taking your business idea and realizing it to success.

Here are some examples of the areas you may need to address when assembling your team:

- **Getting HR administration in place**—Your HR (human resources) needs may be sporadic, ongoing, big, or small depending on the size and structure of your company. HR involves managing employee benefits, payroll and tax administration, healthcare, 401k, training and development, risk management and safety...the list is seemingly never-ending. That's why many entrepreneurs either hire someone to handle the HR in-house or outsource their HR needs to a reputable service provider such as a PEO (professional employer organization). Find the solution that makes sense for your business and your budget.

- **Building your dream team**—Building a business is typically a team effort. You might have the need for full-time employees, part-time employees, independent contractors, vendors and suppliers, business advisors, business partners, or professional allies. I've already spent a good amount of time discussing strategies for building your team in a previous chapter, so I won't beat this point into the ground. However, remember to get help where you need it, find people whose strengths can compensate for your weaknesses, and get others to complete the tasks that you don't have time for or that aren't directly making you money.

## Technology

Technology drives today's businesses. Smart entrepreneurs know how to select the right technology to help them achieve more with less effort, less time, and less money. With the right technology, your business will run more efficiently, require less ongoing upkeep, and even look bigger and more professional.

Setting up your technology is a process you need to take very seriously. There is so much great technology out there that can help you make your business run more efficiently and more profitably. When developing your business, you need to focus on setting up the technological infrastructure of your company, including such as your computers, smart phones, software applications, business project management tools, website, data backup and protection, etc. Don't treat this step lightly. The right technology can make your day easier and make you faster and better at what you do. The wrong technology, on the other hand, can cause your company to be slow, ineffective, disorganized, and unprofitable; it can also create very serious security risks.

Take the time to choose the right vendors so you can enjoy better services at the best prices. Phone and Internet companies are constantly fighting with one another to try to win business customers. By keeping on top of the latest promotional offers and service plans, you can find the best deal, saving you money on the services your business uses on a daily basis.

The Internet is your best friend when it comes to researching and acquiring the right technology for your business. But if you're not technically inclined and setting up an IT infrastructure is completely foreign to you, don't be afraid to enlist outside help from an expert so that you can put together a smart network that drives your business forward.

**Market**

Market research is a critical part of this phase in the Roadmap. It involves everything from researching your target customers so you can dig down to better understand their wants, needs, and desires to actually further developing your products and services so you can bring them to market. Without a doubt, this is one of the most important components of the entire Roadmap because it is directly linked to sales and your bottom line.

- **Customer research**—You must know thy customer. Understanding your customer will help ensure you hit the mark with them when it comes time to launch your products and services. There are many methods you can use to research your customers, including time-tested, traditional methods like surveys and focus groups as well as budget-saving, creative methods like tapping social media and discussion lists to working with a local university to get your business used as a real-life market research project for their students.

- **Developing your products and services**—Of course, you can't have a business without having a product or service to sell. So, you need to completely develop whatever it is that you're selling. Remember, the marketing is in the product. If the product isn't great, no amount of sales and marketing will make you successful. A bad product or service will always fail at some point. Developing your product is a detailed process that involves careful testing, analysis, and refinement. You do not want to rush your product to market before it's ready, because a bad product launch can be the death of a new company. You have to test thoroughly and work out as many of the kinks as you can now so that as you launch your business, your product is the best it can be.

## Management

As an entrepreneur, there are many different areas that require your attention and ongoing management. I've already spent a great deal of time in this chapter and throughout this book discussing business management, but you must also focus on managing yourself, various business projects, risk, and relationships:

- **Personal management**—Managing yourself is one of the hardest things you'll have to do. You need to know how to manage your time effectively. That means knowing which tasks you need to focus on, getting them done efficiently, and also making time for your personal life. This is a topic we touched on extensively in the Time and Effort chapter earlier in this book, so I suggest you refer back to that if you need more guidance in personal management.

- **Project management**—In managing your business, there are countless smaller projects that demand your attention, such as developing your products and services, raising capital, marketing, sales, and so on. Effective project management is about being organized, having clear objectives, creating a sound strategy and plan for achieving those objectives, and tracking your progress carefully. Remember, don't be afraid to delegate projects to trusted individuals, especially projects that aren't essential to growing your bottom line.

- **Risk management**—Being an entrepreneur is about taking risks. Risk management is a huge topic; in fact, I've already devoted an entire chapter to it. You need to have a tolerance for taking risks, but at the same time, you have to be smart and calculated in the risks you take. There are smart risks and dumb risks. You need to assess all risks thoroughly and always be prepared for the unexpected.

- **Relationship management**—Savvy entrepreneurs know how to create and maintain good relationships. From your personal relationships with your family and friends to professional relationships with employees, contractors, vendors, and customers, you're going to have to spend time cultivating and nurturing all different kinds of relationships. While each relationship is different, you should remember that every relationship is built on trust and communication. If you focus on these two areas, you can succeed at relationship management.

Again, these are major areas of focus that the roadmap helps you through and some of the steps you will need to take when establishing your business. What's important at this time is that you put the right focus on the right things. Stay out of the weeds. Stay on track. So many things could be said about the value of this phase of the Roadmap. One of the greatest entrepreneurs was Steve Jobs. He has been described as being a person that had intense determination, was laser-focused, and was always looking ahead. This is what helped him accomplish great things in business.

Primarily that is what this phase of the Accelerated Entrepreneur Roadmap helps the entrepreneur to do at a time when there is danger of getting bogged down. It is a framework to keep you focused on key areas of establishing the business, and it offers a way for you to be looking ahead, so you can follow through and reach your payday.

## 5th Phase: Rapid to Cash

Now comes the best part. All of the work the entrepreneur has done in each phase thus far in identifying, developing, and establishing their business is about to come to fruition. It's time to start making money! Of course, I don't want you to think that all of the hard work is over. On the contrary, there is still plenty of work to be done if you want your business to be profitable and successful, but at this point on the Accelerated Entrepreneur Roadmap, you're at the stage where you're ready to start selling your product or service to customers so you can begin realizing your dream to be a successful entrepreneur. It's the Rapid to Cash phase (doesn't that just sound exciting?).

However, something you have to realize is that just having a great, unique product or service isn't going to make you successful. There have been many good products from good companies that have flopped horribly. In fact, 80 percent of new product launches fail, according to *Forbes*. History is replete with examples of failed products, from New Coke to Sony Betamax.

How can you keep your product and your company from suffering the same fate? By utilizing this Rapid to Cash approach in this final phase of the Accelerated Entrepreneur Roadmap, you can quickly improve your odds of earning a profit. It uses as input the important base of knowledge and experience you have built up in the previous phases of work and then focuses on the most important components of turning your product or service into cash. It leads you step-by-step to realizing commercialization of your business by building out and refining your marketing strategy and plan, launching your business products/services with effective campaigns, promotions, and pricing strategies, and managing your sales.

In an effort to help you get your business turning a profit so you can bridge the Valley of Death that kills so many startups, here are some of the components of this crucial phase.

## Marketing

Your business won't survive if you can't make a sale. It's as simple as that. You need to be obsessed with getting leads, converting leads into sales, generating referral business, keeping existing customers happy, and earning repeat sales from your customers.

Without customers, your business will fail. Never lose sight of this simple fact, and don't allow yourself to become distracted by things that won't make you money and keep your company alive. Create a marketing and sales funnel system that you can use to get leads and make sales.

When planning your marketing strategy, make sure you're doing just that: *planning*. That means you need to have clearly defined goals that you want to achieve with your marketing efforts, and you need to have a strategy in place for achieving those goals. In other words, you must define the "what" and the "how" so that you have a vision and aren't flying by the seat of your pants.

The good news is that there are many low-cost, easy-to-implement marketing tactics you can use to build buzz for your brand and drive traffic. Some of these methods include social media marketing (connecting with your target customers on Facebook, Twitter, etc.), email marketing, pay-per-click advertising, public relations, referral marketing, and so much more. With all the tools and technology entrepreneurs now have at their disposal, there's no excuse for not getting the word out about your products and services. If you don't know how to do this, enlist the help of a professional that does.

**Product/Service Launch**

Simply having a great product or service isn't a guarantee that you'll be successful. You must launch your product or service in such a way that it grabs the attention of your target audience, gets them motivated to buy, makes them tell others about your product and service, and keeps them coming back for more. A poorly executed product or service launch can be difficult to bounce back from, so you must do everything you can to get off to a great start.

Here are some of the things you need to keep in mind during your launch:

- **Focus on the customer**—Yes, your product or service has lots of great features and bells and whistles. But guess what? Your customers don't really care about all of those details. What they care about is how it affects them. How is your product or service going to make your customer's life better? How will they benefit by using it? What problems will it solve for them? This is how you need to frame your marketing when launching your product or service.

- **Get influencers on board early on**—Every industry has thought leaders and influencers. For instance, when a tech company is getting ready to release a new, cutting-edge gadget, they often provide leading tech bloggers and journalists with a presentation on the new product or they even send them the product before release so they can test it out for themselves and review it for their readers. This builds buzz and gets the general public excited.

- **Make your product launch an event**—When Apple launches a new product, the world knows about it. They really do it up big and have a huge event. Before his death, CEO Steve Jobs used to be out there center stage giving an amazing, spellbinding presentation showcasing the new product and getting everyone excited. So, if you have the budget, consider hosting a significant press event for the launch of your new product or service. If a smaller budget, maybe you could hold an online, virtual event. The point is to make as big a deal as possible of your product or service launch so that people will notice and take it seriously.

You only get one chance to launch a new product or service. You have to really make it count. Don't be afraid to pull out all the stops, because a successful product or service launch can truly make your company successful now and for years to come. Start planning early so that all the pieces are in place when it comes time to release your product or service to the masses.

## Commercialization Realization

Once your product or service is released, it's time to start making money. It's time to see all that hard work and research you've done to date manifest itself in the form of cold, hard cash.

During the commercial realization step of the Rapid to Cash phase on the Accelerated Entrepreneur Roadmap™, you should keep these following tips in mind:

- **Get cash flowing as quickly as possible**—Many businesses fail early on because they just can't get the cash flowing in quickly enough to bridge "The Valley of Death." The Valley of Death is the gap between when a business idea is conceived and the point at which it becomes profitable. It's the point where the entrepreneur has exhausted all capital and doesn't have enough cash flow to keep the business alive. What can you do to expedite cash flow in the early stages of launching your company? For service-based businesses, you can request deposits upfront on all work and request payment for the rest of the work upon delivery. You can even do this if you develop products. From highly anticipated video games due to be released later in the year to limited edition automobiles that are in the manufacturing process, there are all types of products that consumers are willing to place deposits down on in advance of receiving it.

- **Avoid the temptation to discount**—To start making sales as soon as possible, you might be tempted to slash the prices of your products. In most cases, you want to discourage this. Why? Because doing so cuts into your profit margins and devalues your products or services. Think about it. If a customer sees your product or service being sold at a 25 percent discount, do you think they would ever be willing to pay full price for it in the future? No, because they've been trained to believe that it's not worth full price; its value is the discounted price in their minds. Instead of discounting your product, find ways to add value to your offering. Think of Apple product launches. What was Steve Jobs talking about on the stage of the product launch events? Not how cheap and discounted they were selling products for but how rich the products were in function and value, always using his noted colloquial term, "One more thing." That's the right focus. Increase the value of your product with low-cost or no-cost extras that help you differentiate your product and build goodwill with your customer base.

- **Find ways to drive profits higher**—Your goal should always be to look for new ways to increase your profits. This means finding new leads and new customer segments to target, doing a better job of converting your leads into sales, increasing repeat business, using smart sales and distribution strategies to keep costs low, and increasing the average price point of your sales. It also means finding ways to decrease costs without sacrificing product quality or customer service.

- **Learn from your mistakes**—No matter how prepared you are, you're going to make some mistakes when launching your business. It's inevitable. Challenges will pop up that you aren't prepared for, and there always will be unexpected fires to be put out. That's just what life is like for an entrepreneur. I'm not telling you this to scare you. I'm telling you this to help you get in the right frame of mind for conquering these challenges, overcoming your mistakes, and learning from them so you don't repeat them. Even the most successful entrepreneurs will swing and miss from time to time, but if you're persistent and capable of adapting on the fly, you can succeed.

- **Get a business advisor**—Having an independent, objective business advisor can help you in the launch and operation of your business. A good business advisor will offer objective honest advice, based on experience, knowledge and facts instead of emotions; and a good advisor will hold you accountable to ensure you get the results you desire. Remember, you don't know it all. No entrepreneur has all the answers. We can all use a helping hand and an outside perspective to help us stay on the right path to success.

When you follow the various aspects of the Rapid to Cash phase on the Accelerated Entrepreneur Roadmap, you can develop and increase your customer base, helping you bring in cash now and setting you up to sustain and grow your business over the long term. Remember, many a product or service that seemed to have great potential has failed to launch successfully. Don't get cocky and think your product or service is so great that it will automatically be a smash hit.

It takes work to market and sell your product or service, and it's ongoing work, too. Don't take your foot off the pedal just because the customers start rolling in. You have to keep marketing aggressively to current and to new customers if you want to stay relevant and profitable. Achieving success is only part of the battle; holding on to it is the real challenge.

## Following the Accelerated Entrepreneur Roadmap

As I've said before, starting a business is truly a journey, and without a map to guide you on your journey, you can stray from the path of success and get so lost that you never find your way back.

Countless entrepreneurs have failed because they didn't have a clear roadmap that guided them step-by-step through the process of starting a business.

I truly believe that if you follow the steps in the Accelerated Entrepreneur Roadmap, you can not only significantly increase your chances of being a successful entrepreneur, but you also can increase your chances of achieving that success more quickly instead of on your own without such a framework.

But even with the great framework provided by the Roadmap, it's still helpful to have someone by your side that can help you through each of the phases and their sub-domains, ensuring you stay on track when bringing your business ideas to life. Every entrepreneur can use a helping hand, and that was my inspiration for launching the Accelerated Entrepreneur Lab.

## Accelerated Entrepreneur™ Lab: Helping Entrepreneurs Develop and Grow Their Businesses

An important component of the Accelerated Entrepreneur Roadmap system is the Accelerated Entrepreneur Lab. The Lab is an entrepreneurial innovation center concept providing workshops for entrepreneurs and business-minded individuals to develop and grow entrepreneur and business capabilities.

The Accelerated Entrepreneur Lab fosters an environment where entrepreneurs can identify and develop their business ideas and accelerate toward driving them to fruition and achieving success. Entrepreneurs who attend these Lab sessions can get guidance through the Accelerated Entrepreneur Roadmap, helping them stay on the path to success. These Lab sessions stimulate exploration, innovation, and acceleration, providing valuable interaction that helps entrepreneurs with everything from generating fresh ideas to building out their business concept into reality.

When entrepreneurs attend these workshops, I can work with them directly to help them through their unique challenges, giving them one-on-one guidance so they can overcome barriers standing in their way. Together, we work through the Accelerated Entrepreneur Roadmap, accelerating the entrepreneur toward the success they desire.

From my observation and experience, a dominant trend of our time is the unrelenting, accelerating change in business, and I believe that we can expect that trend to continue for the foreseeable future. Individuals and businesses that fail to utilize a rapid business development approach that accelerates their capabilities will unfortunately be left behind.

To prevent this, there must be an embracing of the challenge to adopt new innovative methods to meet business demand and opportunity. The Accelerated Entrepreneur System provides a needed roadmap and framework that an individual can learn from and practice for their own business success.

I encourage you to visit our website to learn more about the Accelerated Entrepreneur™ Lab and to discover how participating in these sessions can accelerate you to the success you desire. Learn more at www.AcceleratedEntrepreneur.com.

"Enthusiasm can only be aroused by two things: first, an ideal, with takes the imagination by storm, and second, a definite intelligible plan for carrying that ideal into practice"

~ Arnold J. Toynbee, British Historian and Author of The Rise and Fall of Civilizations, A Study of History

# 9

## HOW TO OVERCOME BARRIER #6: LACK OF INDUSTRY AND MARKET KNOWLEDGE

"Knowledge is the antidote to fear."

~ Ralph Waldo Emerson

Suppose you had never seen a baseball game in your entire life. You were completely clueless about how the game was played or what the rules were. You didn't know any of the terminology used in the game—*strike, ball, foul ball, out, home run.*

Now, imagine being thrown out onto the field and asked to play. It would be pretty difficult, don't you think? You wouldn't know which way to run if you got a hit, and you wouldn't know what to do with the ball if you caught it. It would be a disaster, and your chances of having a good game would be nil.

That's what it's like when you start a business without any industry knowledge.

Before I started my business information and service companies focusing on entrepreneurs and businesses, I had spent many years working as a leader in consulting firms. I was fortunate to work as a member of several top tier global consulting firms, and needless to say, I learned a lot along the way. Without the knowledge and experience I had previously gained through that, I wouldn't have been in as good a position to start my own business information and coaching companies. Simple as that.

I leveraged the industry knowledge I gained over those years to help me start my own successful businesses. It provided me insights to where I could know where opportunities existed, how I could take advantage of them, what I could do differently than others in the business, and what I needed to do to be competitive. This business knowledge has proven to be my most valuable asset as an entrepreneur.

## A Major Barrier to Entrepreneurs

According to the Kauffman survey, lack of industry knowledge is one of the top challenges faced by founders in starting a business. 83 percent of the founders surveyed said that knowledge about industry and markets were important barriers entrepreneurs faced. These experienced entrepreneurs were emphatically stating that lack of knowledge about the industry and markets was a very important factor that actually prevented others from becoming entrepreneurs.

This really isn't all that surprising when you think about it. Doing something as daunting as starting your own business without knowing anything about the industry or markets is pretty darn scary, don't you think? When you don't know something, doubt creeps in. That voice inside your head starts telling you that you can't do it. It tells you that you're not smart enough or experienced enough to start your own business. It tells you that you're better off giving up, that maybe you're not really cut out to be an entrepreneur.

It's the fear of the unknown that is the most crippling fear of them all.

Of course, what many would-be entrepreneurs seem to be failing to realize is that all knowledge is attainable. You can truly learn anything if you set your mind to it, especially in this day and age where information is more accessible than ever before. But before I share some of the different ways you can go about acquiring knowledge about particular industries, let's take a closer look at why it's so dangerous to start a business without industry knowledge.

## The Dangers of Starting a Business Without Industry Knowledge

I'm a firm believer in the power of knowledge-driven entrepreneurship. It just makes sense to start a business in an industry that you know. If you try to start a business without understanding the industry that you're going to be operating in, you're setting yourself up for failure. Lack of knowledge about an industry means that you won't understand what challenges you might face, what opportunities might exist, and what general environment you'll be working in.

These aren't the only disadvantages of having a lack of industry knowledge. If you're planning on raising capital through investors, your lack of industry knowledge and experience could prevent you from securing the money you need. Many investors believe and understand that a business is more likely to succeed if the parties involved have experience and knowledge in the industry they are pursuing. Therefore, investors want to see that you know your industry and your business and will be able to leverage that knowledge and experience to make your company successful.

In addition, starting a business without industry knowledge can prove challenging from an organizational standpoint. Lack of experience can lead to poor organization of a company and its resources. Your lack of knowledge could mean that you don't understand how a business in the particular industry needs to be setup to operate efficiently and profitably. It's like trying to build a house without a blueprint.

Another danger of starting a business without industry or market knowledge is that it can lead to you being overly ambitious and too optimistic. Don't misunderstand me. I'm all for optimism. I think it's an important trait for entrepreneurs to have. But that optimism has to be grounded in reality and a solid foundation of knowledge.

Unfortunately, too many times entrepreneurs are overly optimistic about their business ideas. They get an idea, think it's guaranteed to succeed, and rush in without ever stopping to truly explore the opportunity, understand the industry they'll be working in, and probe the marketplace to determine if the idea really has legs. This is why I have steps in the Accelerated Entrepreneur Roadmap where after you complete your evaluations, you take your business ideas through the needed steps of exploring and evolving them to confirm if they are viable and have potential for success...before spending your valuable resources of time and money on something half-baked.

In the end, it's this extreme optimism born from their lack of industry knowledge that is the undoing for some. If such an entrepreneur had taken the time to learn about the industry and market, they might have realized that their idea was unrealistic or needed to be tweaked in order to be successful.

## Experience: A Great Teacher

C.S. Lewis said, "Experience: that most brutal of teachers. But you learn, my God do you learn."

You can read all the books in the world to prepare yourself for starting a business in a particular industry, but until you actually get out there and do it, you'll never completely learn everything that you need to know. Real world experience is the best teacher you can have.

That's why many entrepreneurs tend to start businesses in industries that they have prior experience in.

Before founding the successful chain of burrito restaurants Chipotle, Steve Ells worked as a sous chef under Jeremiah Tower at Stars restaurant in San Francisco. He got the itch to start his own Mexican restaurant inspired by the taco shops he used to frequent around the city. He wanted to start a restaurant that offered the convenience of fast food but with a totally redefined experience.

So, Ells borrowed money from his parents, and put his industry experience to work when he founded his first Chipotle in Denver in 1993. Nearly 20 years later, there are about 1,000 Chipotle restaurants, and the company doesn't seem to be showing any signs of slowing down.

Along the way, Ells was named Rocky Mountain News Business Person of the Year in 2005, and in 2007 he received the CEO of the Year Award from *ColoradoBiz* magazine. His expertise was also put to use as he joined the judging and investment panel on NBC's TV show *America's Next Great Restaurant*.

But Ells certainly isn't the only entrepreneur to put his prior industry experience and knowledge to work when launching a new business. Consider Jim Koch, founder of The Boston Beer Company, the company behind Samuel Adams beer.

You could joke that beer runs through Koch's veins rather than blood, and you wouldn't be far from the truth. Koch's father was a fifth-generation brewer, but he left the business when the big brewers started to use mass production techniques. So, Jim Koch grew up and got a job as a management consultant, but in 1984, he saw a business opportunity, dug out his great-great grandfather's recipe, and began brewing beer in his kitchen.

Koch was able to leverage his family's extensive industry experience to help his company become the nation's largest craft-beer brewer. The company is incredibly profitable, and much of this can be credited to the Koch family's experience in the beer industry.

As an entrepreneur advisor, I encourage budding entrepreneurs to take a cold, hard look at their experience. I have them examine the industries they've worked in, because often times, this experience gives them a better understanding of how to start a successful business in a particular field.

When you have extensive experience working in an industry, you can leverage that experience to:

- Identify business opportunities that others are overlooking

- Use your industry connections and resources to help get your business off the ground

- Structure your business in a way that has been proven to work in the industry

- Avoid common mistakes that you've seen others make in the industry

Simply put, industry experience can increase your chances of overcoming the many barriers that entrepreneurs face, and according to SmallBizTrends.com, "various dimensions of start-up performance – survival, sales growth, employment growth, and profitability all increase with the number of years of experience that an entrepreneur has in the industry in which he or she is starting a business."

As you're reading this right now, I want you to pause for a moment to consider your professional experience. Is there a particular industry you have experience in? If so, this could be fertile ground to think of business ideas and opportunities that would be a great fit for you in that industry.

## When NOT to Start a Business in an Industry You Have Experience In

Now, before you commit yourself to starting a business in an industry you've been working in for years, I have to mention that there is a certain situation in which you should not start a business in an industry you have experience in.

If the industry is not favorable to start-ups, you probably don't want to try to start a business because the chances of failure are going to be high. Not all industries are welcoming to entrepreneurs. The failure rates of businesses vary widely by industry, so if your experience lies in an industry with high business failure rates, you might want to steer clear.

Using data from the Census Bureau's Business Dynamic Statistics, Scott Shane at SmallBizTrends.com studied the 5 year survival rates for new companies founded in 2005. The survival rates by industry are listed below, in order from the highest to lowest:

- Mining (51.3 percent)

- Manufacturing (48.4 percent)
- Services (47.6 percent)
- Wholesaling and Agriculture (47.4 percent)
- Retailing (41.1 percent)
- Finance, Insurance, and Real Estate (39.6 percent)
- Transportation, Communications and Utilities (39.4 percent)
- Construction (36.4 percent)

So, for example, if you've spent the last 10 years of your life working in the construction industry, now may not be the best time for you to use that experience to start a business in construction. The survival rates are just so low that, even with all your industry experience and knowledge, you'd probably have a hard chance of succeeding, unless you truly had a revolutionary, industry-changing business idea.

## No Experience Necessary? The Difference Between Experience and Knowledge

So, if one has no industry experience or all of their experience is an industry that's hostile to startups, does that mean they can't be an entrepreneur? Not at all!

There are many successful entrepreneurs who have started business in industries that they had no prior experience in whatsoever.

Consider the story of Magic Johnson. Basketball fans remember him for his amazing set of skills displayed on the court during his Hall of Fame career. But I'm personally far more impressed with Magic's work off the court as an entrepreneur.

When he was in the seventh year of his basketball career, Magic started to seriously think about what he would do after his playing days were over. He had seen countless athletes fail to adapt to life after the game, and he refused to be another failure story.

So, Magic set up a meeting with a powerful executive by the name of Michael Ovitz, co-founder of Creative Artists Agency. At that meeting, Ovitz told Magic to start reading the business section of the newspaper every day. If Magic wanted to start a successful business empire, he would have to learn about business.

Decades later, Magic Johnson Enterprises now owns or operates movie theatres, gyms, coffee shops, electronics retail outlets, and other businesses in many cities across the country. He's now even a part owner of the Major League baseball team the Los Angeles Dodgers. In 2009, *Ebony* magazine said that Magic Johnson was one of the most influential black business leaders in America.

Now, before you start thinking that Magic Johnson is a special case because he had the connections that come with being a celebrity, I want to tell you another story of successful entrepreneurs who started a business in an industry they knew nothing about.

Timothy Ericson and Jason Meinzer started CityRyde (now called Zagster), a bike-sharing consulting firm in 2007 with no prior domain experience. As Ericson told *Entrepreneur* magazine, "We started from nothing. We basically spent our first two years becoming experts in an industry that was totally new to us."

Ericson spent two years meeting with and learning from different bike-sharing companies around the world. This helped him understand how the industry worked, its best practices, what opportunities were available, and what he needed to do to make CityRyde successful in this niche.

Ericson went on to explain, "Before we started CityRyde, there was very little general knowledge available about the industry. So we went out and obtained that knowledge directly from the vendors to find out what they needed to be successful in this growing industry."

The company is now highly influential in the industry, and all of its success comes in spite of its owners having no prior industry experience.

Clearly, starting a successful business is possible in an industry you have no previous experience in, but as the two stories above clearly demonstrate, gaining knowledge about an industry is the key to success. Magic spent years reading about business; Ericson went around the world to study the bike-sharing industry.

If you want to be successful, you have to put in the time to gain the knowledge about the industry your business will be operating in. It could take significant time for you to learn about an industry, but if you're willing to put in the hard work of researching and studying an industry, you can be successful even without prior domain experience.

I've mentioned it already a few times, but the savviest entrepreneurs are fanatical about learning. They have an insatiable thirst for knowledge, and they're always committed to doing whatever it takes to learn more, so they can be better, wealthier entrepreneurs.

## How to Learn About an Industry

Now, we arrive at the real core of this important barrier. If an entrepreneur lacks industry knowledge, what can he or she do to remedy the situation? In other words, how does one go about learning about an industry?

Over the next several pages, we'll touch on several different ways you can gain knowledge about an industry you're exploring. Undoubtedly, there may be some techniques and avenues for gaining industry knowledge that go unmentioned or get glossed over, but my purpose isn't to exhaustively detail every possible method you can use to learn about an industry. Instead, my goal is to highlight what I believe are some strategies you can use to learn about an industry, and more importantly, I want to help you get in a mindset where you're empowered to seek out knowledge, wherever it might be.

## *The 3 R's Approach to Learning About an Industry*

The approaches one can take to learn about an industry fall under what I like to call the 3 R's. No, I'm not talking about reading, 'riting, and 'rithmetic. I'm talking about Research, Relationships, and Recognition. Research is about the sources and methods to utilize in learning about an industry and markets. Relationships are about identifying those to connect with relative to the industry and how to exploit those connections. Recognition is about the importance of recognizing trends and spotting opportunities. Each of the various methods for acquiring industry knowledge that I'm going to detail in this chapter will fit into one of these categories.

## *Research*

I remember back in college when I'd get an assignment to write a huge research paper on a particular subject. Back in those days, we didn't have the Internet, so researching a topic meant going to the library and digging up as many books, newspaper articles, and magazine articles as I could on the particular subject. I had to spend hours and hours reading through all of the various books, newspapers, and magazines to learn as much as I could about the subject matter so I could write a well thought out paper.

This isn't all that different from the approach you can take when trying to learn about an industry. Look, you aren't going to become an industry expert by osmosis. This isn't like the movie named *The Matrix*; you can't just download the knowledge into your brain and instantly become all knowing about a particular industry.

No, it takes lots and lots of research. And that means lots and lots of reading. As Confucius once said, "No matter how busy you may think you are, you must find time for reading, or surrender yourself to self-chosen ignorance."

Ignorance kills entrepreneurs.

So, what exactly should you be reading when doing your research?

- **Books**—I love reading books. I read all different types of business, marketing, and consulting books, and I use the information I absorb from these books to improve my entrepreneurial skills and to improve my business and the services I offer to my customers. No matter what industry you're in, there are certainly many books written on the subject. Find them; read them. Don't know of any good industry books off the top of your head? What I like to do is go to Amazon.com, search for your books in a particular industry, read reviews of the various books to see which ones are best, and when it's available, click the "Look Inside" option to take a peek into the book to get a better idea of what it's about. I also do Google searches for books in specific industries as well. Also there is still the opportunity to peruse bookstores and libraries for beneficial information. Opportunities abound.

- **Blogs and social media**—There are millions of blogs on the web. Literally. You can be sure there are plenty of blogs devoted to your industry, various companies in your industry, products, etc. There are a lot of great things about reading blogs. First, it gives you the absolute latest information regarding your industry. If something important happens today in your industry, you can be sure that there will be blog posts about it within hours, so it's a great way to stay in the loop. Another great thing is that reading different blogs gives you access to a range of different opinions and perspectives. This helps open your mind, and it allows you to see things from all different angles, so you can formulate your own thoughts and opinions. Use Google Blog Search or Technorati to find the different blogs in your field. And while you're at it, connect with industry thought leaders and your target audience through social networking, on LinkedIn, Facebook, Twitter, or whatever the hot social networking site is at the moment.

- **Industry news and publications**—Every industry has various trade publications and news resources devoted to it. These publications share the latest industry news, thoughts and analysis, information about trends, and so much more, helping you gain the knowledge you need to stay competitive in the marketplace. How can you find industry, trade and business publications? There are certain websites out there that are helpful for identifying publications and that even provide free information on them in certain cases. You could begin by checking out current examples such as these: TradePub.com,

FreeTradeMagazineSource.com, and Bizjournals.com. For example Bizjournals.com, not only has national information but also specific journals by city where you can find local business directories as well as information on local industry conventions and trade shows. To branch out further, sites as Tsnn.com and Biztradeshows.com provide industry information for trade shows and conventions in the U.S. and across countries. Of course you can also do a simple Google search for "(industry name) trade journal" or "(industry name) trade publication."

- **Product and service reviews**—Every marketplace has competition, and the better you know your competitors' strengths and weaknesses, the better you'll be able to position yourself advantageously against them. I like reading descriptions and reviews of the various products and services in the niche I'm competing in. This gives me great insight into what my target audience thinks about the products and services my competitors are providing. I can see what customers like and see what they dislike, so I can improve my own products and services to better match their needs. Reading product and service descriptions and reviews also helps you stay current on the latest product features in your industry so that you're not getting left behind.

- **Corporate reports**—Annual corporate reports are an excellent resource for learning about specific companies in your industry as well as gaining general industry information. Corporate reports often cover the state of the industry, market share information, government regulations, industry concerns, and more. By reading corporate reports from different companies in your industry, you can easily identify common themes and issues that are affecting companies in the industry. Many companies now publish their corporate reports directly on their website. You can also find them online at sites as AnnualReports.com, AnnualReportService.com, and Hoovers.com. You can also contact companies directly to request their annual reports.

- **Regulatory information and legal issues**—A lot of industries are heavily regulated and have many important legal issues that affect businesses. Understanding the various regulatory issues and laws will help you to first determine if it's worth starting a business in the industry and also to make sure that your business is fully compliant. One way to discover these issues is to read the corporate reports of various companies in the industry. Above, I mentioned how you can access these reports. You can also search Lexis Nexis databases for information which can be available at many academic libraries or at their online retail websites. Also there is Justia.com which provides free legal and regulation information and is searchable by industry and company. Don't forget your state and local government public information databases that are available as well. As for regulatory issues, depending on the industry you're in, you'll want to explore information provided by the EPA, OSHA, and Better Business Bureau as a start. Also, the Library of Congress offers a great online resource for searching current legislation in Congress so you can stay current on proposed and recent regulations. You can search online at Thomas.loc.gov.

- **Patents and trademarks**—Patents, copyrights, and trademarks are very important in just about every industry. You want to make sure your idea is truly original, that your intellectual property is protected, and that you're not infringing on anyone else's intellectual property. Thankfully, the Internet makes searching for patents and trademarks fairly easy. To search for patents and trademarks, you can visit the United States Patent and Trademark Office's website at USPTO.gov. The site has a section for searching its full text and image patent database, and also a section for trademark information and electronic searches. Likewise, for copyright information and record searches you can go to the U.S. Copyright Office at Copyright.gov.

- **Advertisements**—Take a look at how other companies in your industry are advertising and marketing themselves. What types of products and services are they pushing? What are the key features and benefits of these products and services that are being touted in the advertisements? The point of this exercise isn't so that you can mimic exactly what everyone else is doing. The point is to help you get an idea of what's trending in the marketplace right now, and so you can identify gaps and opportunities where you can fit your products and services in a unique way.

- **Training materials**—Online seminars, classes, and training materials provide a great way for you to learn about any industry and get your knowledge and skill set where they need to be in order for you to operate in that space. Apple's iTunes University is a great place to find tons of lectures, films, and videos on just about every topic you can imagine. They literally offer hundreds of thousands of resources on a huge range of industries, and a lot of the stuff they offer is free. Again, you can also do a simple web search to track down training materials in your industry. Some web searches to consider are: "(industry name) online training"; "(industry name) online seminars"; "free (industry name) online classes."

Again, all of these things are just a starting point for your industry education. When you get in the learning mindset, you'll be able to find information in a range of different places. It might be in the transcript of an interview from an industry thought leader or it might be in a blog post from a consumer. Information is all around us. Keep your eyes, ears, and mind open at all times.

We live in a time where there is no excuse for ignorance. The information is out there, and more accessible than ever before. Don't have a lot of money to spend? There's still tons of free information available all over the Internet. You don't have to spend a lot or even anything at all to start learning about an industry. All you need is an Internet connection and a commitment to soaking up all the knowledge you possibly can.

I also want to point out that while the bulk of your initial learning will be done in the early days of exploring your business idea, your education should never stop. Don't get comfortable and think you know everything there is to know about an industry. Things are always changing, and he who stops learning will get left behind.

Set aside time each day for reading about your industry. Your knowledge will always be your biggest asset.

## *Relationships*

When discussing his initial business meeting with agent Michael Ovitz, Magic Johnson said one of the biggest lessons he learned was that "if you want to be successful, you have to be willing to use every connection you've got."

In other words, it's not always what you know, it's who you know that matters, too.

Trying to learn about an industry all on your own is a monumental task. You can only gain so much information from all the various research you do, and that's why it's important to have a great network in place as well.

You should focus your efforts on developing relationships in the industry with other business owners, buyers, vendors, distributors, and others who have great inside knowledge about the industry.

How can you do this?

- **Look at who you already know**—Oftentimes, our best people resources are hiding in plain sight. This is especially true if you've been working in an industry for a long time. If you have a lot of experience working in the industry, chances are you already know a lot of people whose knowledge could be useful to you. It might be former co-workers, employers, customers, vendors, or just about anyone else you met during your career. Take a close look at your network as it stands right now. Identify the people who could be of use to you, and focus your efforts on improving those relationships. Just like any other type of relationship, it takes work to maintain and grow these business relationships. It takes communication. It takes some give and take. But if you put in the relationship management work, you can leverage other people's knowledge to help you start and grow your business.

- **Attend networking events**—Unless you live out in a rural area far from towns with no one else around, I'm willing to bet there are some business networking events held in your area on a regular basis. You need to be out there attending these events so you can grow your network and meet people who can help you increase your industry knowledge and improve your business. Now, I want to point out that not all networking events are worth attending. Some networking groups just won't have any people that will be of benefit to you. Others might be too cliquish and difficult for you to make any meaningful connections. To determine if a networking event is worth attending, you need to first identify what your goals are. Who are you looking to meet? Are those people likely to be at the event? If not, don't waste your time. Also, I want to warn you to make sure you're not spending too much time at networking events. Yes, these events can be very useful for growing your network, but sometimes, we use them as nothing more than an excuse to get out of the office and avoid work. That's why I recommend setting aside a specific amount of time for attending these events each month. Stay focused and make the right connections.

- **Use social media**—Don't have time to get out and meet people face to face? Too shy for networking events? Looking for a way to quickly meet lots of new people and improve the relationships you already have? Social media is truly a heaven send. Using Twitter, Facebook, LinkedIn, and other social networking sites, you can connect with key people throughout your industry. Not only can you learn a lot about an industry just by paying attention to the things these people post, but you can also interact with them and start building true relationships that could be very profitable for starting and growing your own business. You could gain customers this way or even possibly meet a business partner. The power of social networking is truly remarkable.

- **Go to trade shows**—Attending trade shows is a great way to learn about an industry, identify the different companies and vendors working within an industry, see what's trending and where the industry is headed, and of course, grow your network. You can meet reps from many of the companies in your industry, vendors, buyers, customers, and all sorts of other people. TSNN.com and BizTradeShows.com are both examples of websites for finding trade shows and events in various industries.

- **Join trade organizations**—Every industry has its own organizations and associations. Becoming a member of the right trade organizations will not only help you make useful industry connections, but it can also give you exclusive access to information (studies, industry data, etc.) that's only available to members. Typically, trade organizations and associations will have a website, so you can identify the various trade groups in your industry by searching the web for "(industry name) trade associations" or "(industry name) trade organizations." Most will cost money to join, so do your research to identify which organizations will be the most profitable for you to join.

- **Listen to Customers**—You've undoubtedly heard the phrase, "The customer is always right." Debate it all you want, but at the end of the day, the success of your business is in the hands of your customers. Don't you think it makes sense to actually listen to them? Listening to the voice of the customers is one of the best ways you can learn about an industry. You need to talk to your target audience and see what products and services they'd be interested in, what features they desire, what they like and dislike about your competitors products and services, and what they feel companies in the industry are overlooking. Starting a business or continuing to run a business without listening to the customers is incredibly dangerous. If you're not listening to the customers, you'll simply be guessing as to whether or not they'll actually want what you offer, and with so much at stake, you can't afford to rely on guesswork.

- **Learning from a Business Mentor and Coach—** Working with a business mentor and coach can be a good way to learn about an industry, explore business ideas, assess industry opportunities, and get your business off the ground and headed in the right direction. Of working with a business mentor, Magic Johnson said, "If you want someone to be your mentor, you better be ready to listen and be humbled. Michael (Ovitz) wasn't sure about working with me because so many athletes think they can move right into business and never take anyone's advice. I had to prove to him I was serious and that I would listen." You can't learn from someone else if you don't have your ears and mind open. You have to accept that you don't know everything and give your advisor the opportunity to help you increase your industry knowledge.

## *Recognition*

Recognition is all about taking all of the industry information that you soak up and using it to identify entrepreneurial opportunities in the industry. Just as importantly, it's about recognizing which opportunities and industries are dead ends.

For example, if during your research, you discover that new regulations are being placed on an industry that make it difficult for businesses to operate profitably, you would hopefully recognize that it's not a good idea to start a business in that industry right now.

On the other hand, during your researching and relationship managing, you might discover that all of the companies in a particular industry are overlooking a certain segment of customers or failing to meet a specific need of their current customers. In this situation, you'd need to recognize that there was an opportunity to start a business or launch a product or service that met this unfulfilled need.

It's important to point out that opportunities are not the same as ideas. Just because you have a business idea doesn't necessarily mean that a valid business opportunity exists. Your idea might not be possible to execute or there may not be a market for it.

A true opportunity is one that is based on a product, service, or business idea that creates and adds value for the consumer, that is sustainable, that can be implemented in a profitable way, and that can be implemented at the right time.

Timing might just be the most important thing to focus on here. Sometimes, ideas are too far ahead of their time, and the market just isn't ready for them. Other times, you come up with an idea a little too late, and your competitors have a jump on you.

It's all about recognizing the window of opportunity. Once there's a need for a new product, service, or business idea, its window of opportunity in the market just opens up. You have to be able to enter that window of opportunity before too many others do, causing the market to mature, decline, and the window of opportunity to slam closed.

Now, how exactly do you go about recognizing an industry opportunity? In the last chapter, I spent quite a bit of time discussing this in the phases of the Accelerated Entrepreneur Roadmap, so instead of rehashing, I'll point out a few specific things you should be doing:

- **Pay attention to industry trends**—You should always be following trends in your industry and analyzing them so you can understand how these trends are creating new business opportunities. But how do you identify the trends in your industry? One way is to follow the news of your industry very closely. Doing so will allow you to recognize themes and the general direction of your industry. You can also use tools as Google Trends to identify major news events and themes for specific industries and companies over the last couple of years. Another way to identify industry trends is to purchase forecasts and market analysis from independent research firms. Market forecasts project the future of your industry. They project future numbers, trends, challenges, and other characteristics of your particular market. Studying these can help you recognize current and future opportunities so you can get a jump on the competition.

- **Identify the problems of your target audience**—The Research and Relationship categories of the 3 R's approach to industry learning both have components that rely heavily on listening to customers. Listen for their three P's – pains, problems, or predicaments. This is where you can recognize and understand an industry problem and develop an opportunistic solution. From reading product and service feedback to actually taking the time to survey and speak with customers and your target audience, there are many ways you can gain valuable industry knowledge from your customers. The truly important thing is that you use the information you get from your customers to recognize and create business opportunities. If a lot of customers are looking for a particular type of product or service or they want a certain feature in their products and nobody else is providing it, you should recognize that an opportunity may, in fact, exist. Again, it's about having your eyes, ears, and mind open at all times. You can't recognize opportunities if you're not looking and listening for them.

- **Find gaps in the marketplace**—There's a reason small boutique and specialty stores exist and are successful. The reason is that they appeal to a market that is overlooked by mainstream companies. The owners of these boutiques and specialty stores recognized gaps in the marketplace, and they created businesses to fill these gaps. Gaps in the marketplace are created when a product or service is needed by a certain group of people that might not represent a large enough market to be of interest or of profit to larger companies. For example, Spanx was created when Sara Blakely was struggling to find pantyhose that didn't have seamed toes. She needed an undergarment that provided a blemish-free look under her white pants, so she cut the feet off her control top pantyhose and thus the idea for Spanx was formed. Today, Spanx products are available in 41 countries around the world. Blakely recognized that a problem existed that current companies in the industry weren't addressing. So, she created a product that fulfilled that need. You may have to look hard to find these gaps, but if you're always looking and you listen to what customers want, you'll be able to spot these gaps and possibly create a successful business that fills the gaps.

## Industry Disruption with Fresh Innovation

Now, a lot of experts have said that your ability to identify business opportunities increases with the amount of experience you have in a particular industry. The longer you work in an industry, the better you'll be able to see submarkets that are being underserved. You'll also have built a network of colleagues and customers that could provide information that will be key in helping you recognize new opportunities.

While I do agree with this assessment, I also think there's another side that needs to be considered. And that is sometimes a fresh approach to a new industry is what makes opportunities clear. See, if you've been working in a particular industry for years and years, it can be easy to get so consumed with the way things are that you can't see how things could be. You can become trained to think like everyone else in the industry, so you may have your eyes, ears, and mind closed to new opportunities.

So, just because you don't have experience in an industry, don't let yourself be fooled into thinking that you can't spot a good business opportunity. A particular industry and specific market may have been just floating along in its own protective bubble, without any fresh innovation in years. It can be ripe for disruption that creates earnings for the right entrepreneur who has the mix of skills, knowledge, experience, observation, synthesis, etc. that is the trigger for disrupting an industry and creating a winner startup. A fresh set of eyes could help you spot opportunities that the industry veterans are all overlooking.

We have already discussed the barrier that finance can be to entrepreneurs. Yet here is an example of an industry that was controlled by industry veteran companies, set-in-stone expectations, and criteria which were preventing innovation (because they want safe deals) and preventing the dreams of so many from becoming a reality. Then along comes Perry Chen, who is not a finance executive like a CFO but was an artist who wanted to tear down the finance industry's barrier to creativity and expression. He was also aware of the 18th century subscription artist concept that was used by artists and writers of that day to raise money from patrons to fund their books and concerts.

So he founded Kickstarter; a funding platform for creative projects that provided financial support from those in the crowd that desire to support a project. Thus far Kickstarter states that over $350 million has been pledged by more than 2.5 million people funding more than 30,000 creative projects. Kickstarter makes money by charging a reasonable fee if a project funds successfully. It was a new way to finance a project outside of the current industry norms started by someone who was not an experienced industry expert. This kind of fresh innovation can cause significant disruption in a staid industry providing huge opportunity for the entrepreneur.

The main thing is to always be looking for opportunities. It's a mindset...a lifestyle. When you're in that entrepreneurial frame of mind, business ideas and opportunities can just present themselves to you. To recognize them it must become a part of your consciousness to be opportunistic. Just be sure that you put these opportunities and ideas through the Accelerated Entrepreneur Roadmap as a system to verify that they're quality opportunities and you can bring them to fruition. This Roadmap can help entrepreneurs in any industry learn about and generate ideas, recognize and evaluate opportunities, design a business around these opportunities, and realize the business as quickly as possible with a better probability of success.

Also an experienced and knowledgeable business advisor could assist you when entering an industry and help make you more successful in your pursuit of industry knowledge and success in the marketplace. If you think you could use a business advisor, you can find more information at www.successfulentrepreneuradvisor.com.

"The next best thing to knowing something is knowing where to find it."

~ Samuel Johnson

# 10

## HOW TO OVERCOME BARRIER #7: PRESSURES TO KEEP A TRADITIONAL STEADY JOB

"Your time is limited, so don't waste it living someone else's life. Don't be trapped by dogma – which is living with the results of other people's thinking. Don't let the noise of other's opinions drown out your own inner voice. And most important, have the courage to follow your heart and intuition. They somehow already know what you truly want to become."

~ Steve Jobs, co-founder of Apple and Pixar

If you've been an entrepreneur for any significant period of time, you've undoubtedly had at least one person ask you, "So, do you think you're ever going to get a real job?"

Sometimes, these comments are just innocent jokes, and other times, they may be harsh criticism from family members or friends who either don't respect your entrepreneurial endeavors or are seriously concerned about your ability to be successful and to provide for yourself and your family.

You might have thought that the hardest part of being an entrepreneur was related to starting and running your business, but many entrepreneurs find the family and financial pressures to keep a "real" job to be the most challenging barrier to entrepreneurship.

In fact, 73 percent of the entrepreneurs surveyed in the Kauffman study said that family or financial pressures to keep a traditional, steady job were issues that potential entrepreneurs face when starting a business. Some even rated it as a "big challenge" or "extremely big challenge" faced by entrepreneurs.

So many of us know how it feels for family members or friends not to be supportive of our entrepreneurial aspirations. I think for some of them it's because they just don't understand the entrepreneur mentality and heartbeat. Perhaps with others the entrepreneur path does not fit their model of expectations for a career path, and for some they just don't think you can be successful doing it.

Even if they don't come right out and say it, you are always aware of their doubts. You can tell. You know it by the questions they ask or comments made over the course of time you're laboring to overcome challenges to make your business successful. They actually may be stating their doubts or concerns because of how they care for you.

But for the entrepreneur to be successful you can't let them kill the baby (your business idea) you're nurturing in its infancy. You may have to accept that some will never understand, and that you can't be spending your time defending your idea or asking for validation, when you need to focus on taking next steps to move forward. You may have to determine not to tell some your plans and others you may just have to ignore, but for your inner circle that matters in your life you will have to manage it and endeavor to help them help you.

## Your Dreams Don't Pay the Bills

The reason entrepreneurs have to deal with family and financial pressures to keep a traditional, steady job is because dreams alone won't pay the bills. Just because you want to start a business doesn't mean that the bills will stop rolling in until your business begins to turn a profit. You'll still have to pay the mortgage or the rent. You'll still need to pay off the credit cards. You'll still have to pay to fix your car when it breaks down. You'll still have to provide food for yourself and your family, if you have one. If you have kids, they'll still get sick and need to go to the doctor, and you'll have to find a way to pay for that. The bills don't stop!

Simply put—it's expensive to live here on Earth, and if you're trying to start a business and don't have a steady income, you're going to feel the pressure. Many an entrepreneur stays awake at night stressed out from the pressure of trying to provide for themselves and their family. Sometimes, you won't know if or when the next check will come rolling in, and you're left trying to make ends meet some way, somehow.

Remember, the initial capital to fund most ventures comes from personal and family assets, such as savings. So it's not surprising that a lot of entrepreneurs feel pressure from their family to get a traditional job. The idea of dipping into the savings and not having a stable income is scary and even a little crazy to some family members, so it's only natural to get that pressure from them.

Robin Sauve, co-founder of Barkley Logistics, can certainly relate to this. She and her husband John started Barkley Logistics when they bought the assets of Robin's former employer Premier Logistics, which had shut down due to financial difficulty. Robin saw an opportunity to restart the company under a new name and with more efficient operations.

But both she and her husband's parents doubted the venture. Each of their fathers had earned a steady paycheck all their lives and raised their children to understand the importance of financial discipline and having a steady job. John's dad even told them, "Just make sure you have your heads screwed on straight."

The Sauve's have taken financial risks and dealt with both family pressures and financial pressures to keep traditional jobs, but so far, their risks are paying off as the company continues to grow. However, it demonstrates the point that you can't expect everyone to believe in and be as supportive of your entrepreneurial endeavors as you are.

While some of us are blessed to have the love and support of our families to pursue our dreams, others aren't afforded this luxury. These unlucky entrepreneurs have spouses, parents, other relatives, and even friends in their ears saying they need to give up on their dreams and get back to working a "real" job. Starting a successful business is already hard enough as it is. When you add in the additional challenge and burden of an unsupportive family to the mix, you're really facing a steep uphill battle.

## Thrive Under Pressure, But Find Ways to Reduce It

Pressure can be an entrepreneur's greatest motivation. Those who are truly great at what they do thrive under pressure. NBA great Michael Jordan lived for the thrill of having the ball in his hands at the end of the game. Legendary singer-songwriter Jim Croce wrote one of his No. 1 hit singles "Time in a Bottle" the same night his wife told him that she was pregnant because he felt this was his last chance to make music his profession so that he could provide for his family.

When your back is against the wall, you might be able to come up with new ways to make your business successful because you're desperate and success is your only option. Henry Ford's business went broke before he eventually found success with the Ford Motor Company. Donald Trump has filed for bankruptcy in the past, but he found a way to use that financial pressure to motivate him to succeed. The same is true for Walt Disney and countless other entrepreneurs.

So, pressure can make you perform better, and there is something to be said for the added motivation that comes with family and financial pressures to keep a steady job. However, you can't let this pressure go unchecked. It will wear you down over time. If you don't find ways to manage these pressures and reduce them, they could eventually be your undoing.

The good news is that there are many different ways you can reduce the pressures from your personal relationships and your finances. All of the different tactics I'm going to explore in this chapter fall into one of two categories: relationship management (dealing with family) and financial management (keeping yourself from going broke).

### Relationship Management: Dealing with Family Pressures to Keep a Traditional, Steady Job

I'm very fortunate. I have a wife who supports my entrepreneurial dreams and efforts. She gives me all the love, encouragement, and support I need to keep pursuing my business ideas, even when times get tough.

We are an East-meets-West couple. I'm from the USA, and she's an American citizen originally from Vietnam. The reason I mention this is because the Asian culture offers attitudes and behaviors toward family and work that are of a homogenous nature. In other words, work and personal lives are integrated, and thus being supportive to the family is also being supportive to one's work. She is committed to our family and to our success, which means she's committed to the success of the business as well.

I absolutely would not be where I am today without her support. And I can't even begin to explain how appreciative I am to her for it. I know it's not easy to be married to an entrepreneurial individual. The entrepreneurial life is one that's filled with long hours, uncertainty, risk, and stressful moments. But a spouse's support (and the support of others in your immediate family and circle of friends) can really go a long way to helping you persevere.

**Male Entrepreneurs Feel the Pressure to be Breadwinners**

In Kauffman's *The Anatomy of an Entrepreneur: Are Successful Women Entrepreneurs Different From Men?*, we learn that while both male and female entrepreneurs can struggle with the pressure to keep a traditional job, men face this difficulty much more frequently than women. In fact, more than twice as many male entrepreneurs as females cited the family pressure to keep a traditional job as a challenge.

Why is it that men feel this pressure more commonly than women? Personally, I think it's because many have grown up to believe that the man has to provide for his family. As males, many men feel that it's their duty to be the breadwinner in the family.

Therefore, it only makes sense that male entrepreneurs feel the pressure to earn a steady paycheck at a traditional job because they are afraid to fail and not be able to provide for their families. It's important for all entrepreneurs—male and female— to find ways to get the support of their spouse and family so they can overcome this major barrier and see their business idea through to its full potential.

## Women Entrepreneurs Crave Social Support

All entrepreneurs need support from their loved ones. It's incredibly tough to build a business, and it can really wear on you physically, mentally, emotionally and spiritually. It's so very important that you have someone in your corner that can support you and encourage you to get through the hard times. We all need that.

However, in the previously cited Kauffman study of women entrepreneurs, it is revealed that women especially crave and benefit from social support and encouragement. The study reports that "though both sexes rated their professional and business networks as very important to the success of their most recent startups, women emphasized it more. Thus, the role of social capital (defined as the benefits derived from an individual's personal and professional networks) is another key gender difference."

I don't think it's a stretch to say that for many female entrepreneurs the lack of social support could literally be the death of their business. Building a business all on your own is so very hard. We all need some help in one way or another.

## It Ain't Easy Being an Entrepreneur's Spouse or Significant Other

Of course, not all entrepreneurs have the support of their family. And I understand that. Your entrepreneurial endeavors do have a major impact on your family. If your business fails and you go broke, they'll suffer from your failure, too.

There are those who think that being an entrepreneurial spouse or significant other is the greatest thing in the world. They think that because the entrepreneur is their own boss they must make a lot of money and be able to take off work whenever they want to go on vacation or just hang out with the family.

But we know that's not true. Being the significant other of an entrepreneur can be tough. It can be tough being the children of an entrepreneur, too. Despite their best intentions, many entrepreneurs get so caught up with their work that they end up not being the best spouse or parent, and add in the fact that if an entrepreneurial business fails, it can wreck the family's finances.

So I do understand that it's hard for some entrepreneurs to win the support of their family.

However, family support really is a major key to your success. If you have your family riding your backside day in and day out, trying to get you to give up on your business, they're either eventually going to win that fight or it could cause your relationships with family members to fall apart. Neither of these is a good option in my opinion.

## Winning the Support of Your Family

So, the question becomes—How do you win the support of your family? Or at the very least, how do you reduce the amount of pressure they're putting on you to get a "real" job? Much of this revolves around your ability to manage these relationships. You can't let your business turn you into an absentee spouse or family member. You have to be present, and you have to work at managing these relationships and getting your loved ones to share in your dream.

Below, I'm going to outline some specific tactics you can utilize to overcome the very serious barrier of family pressures to keep a traditional job, but as always, my purpose here is not to cover every single imaginable tactic. Instead, I want to help you get in a mindset where you understand how to work with your family to earn their support:

- **Set realistic expectations from the start**—Most businesses take time to be successful and turn a profit. Heck, it takes many businesses a while just to break even. And that's okay, provided that you truly have a sound business idea. If you've put your idea through the Accelerated Entrepreneur Roadmap, not only will you know if your business idea is feasible, but you'll also have a good idea of how long it will take you to break even and then how long it will take before you start turning a profit. This is information you need to share with your family from the beginning. Your spouse and other relatives might not have a lot of business experience, so if they see you struggling early on, they'll think that you're failing. That's when they'll start putting pressure on you to get a real job. But you can manage this by setting clear expectations from the start. Go over your business planning with your family, and let them know the plans and expectations for making money, replacing your current salary, and eventually exceeding your salary.

- **Demonstrate that you truly know your stuff**—Perhaps the most important people you'll have to pitch your business idea to are your immediate family members. Whether you're asking them to invest family financial resources or just to invest their trust and patience, you need to be able to sell them on your idea, and just like when you're pitching investors, the best way to do that is to show them that you know what you're doing. By this point, you should have already done extensive research on your business idea and you should have put it through the early phases of the Accelerated Entrepreneur Roadmap to verify the business opportunity. Now, it's time to share your findings with your family. Put together a presentation for them that details the business opportunity's potential, but don't hide the risks either. If you've worked with a business advisor or mentor that has helped you develop your business model, let your spouse and relatives see that a professional has reviewed and supported your idea. This can go a long way to adding credibility to your entrepreneurial dream.

- **Share stories with them of other successful entrepreneurs**—In many cases, the pressure from family for you to get a traditional job stems from fear that you'll fail. One of the ways to quell that fear is to show your family that other people just like you have taken the entrepreneurial path to success. There are tons of success stories of successful entrepreneurs that you can pull from. I've shared many of them with you throughout this book, and you can find more just by searching the web. Just take a look at some of your favorite companies, or better yet, your spouse or significant other's favorite companies. There's a good chance that the founders of these companies have remarkable stories of overcoming major challenges and defying the odds on their way to success. Share these success stories with your family so you can inspire them and they can see that it is possible to start a successful business.

- **Find out why they don't support you**—Do you know the real reason your family doesn't support you? Is it just about the money? Or are there other issues at play? Maybe your partner is balking because he or she is ready to start a family and doesn't want the uncertainty of entrepreneurship at this point in time. Or maybe your spouse is afraid that you won't have enough time to spend with the family if you're busy trying to run your business. You might think that you know why your family isn't supporting you, but the only way to get to the root of why your family doesn't support you is to talk it out. Don't make assumptions. Sit down with your family and address their feelings and concerns. Don't be defensive. Instead, focus on solutions to these issues, and highlight the benefits of what you're doing for your entire family. Try to see things from their perspective. Communication is absolutely essential. A lot of problems and misunderstandings can be avoided by talking things through. You simply can't have good relationships without good communication.

- **Let them know how they can support you**—In some cases, family pressures and lack of support are simply the result of ignorance. What I mean by that is that your spouse or significant other might not know that they're not supporting you, or they may not know exactly how they can help you. Again, it's all about communication. Express what you want and need from your family. Let them know how much you need their support, and talk about how you're feeling (e.g. scared, tired, lonely, etc.) so they can support you appropriately.

- **Spend quality time with your family every day**—First tier well-known entrepreneur Richard Branson said, "You can and must make time for both family and business. It is important to build a strong family life. It helps to give you a better perspective and balance in business. Moreover, a key responsibility for each generation is to bring up the next generation, and you need to be present to do this." I cannot agree more with Mr. Branson. You absolutely must make time for your family. Building a business does not give you an excuse to not spend time with your spouse and children. Branson also has talked about how spending time with his family actually shaped the way he ran his business. It forced him to learn how to delegate, which is a skill we've talked about quite a bit in this book. Another first tier entrepreneur is that of Elon Musk. He is the exciting entrepreneur in the news behind companies as PayPal, the e-commerce payment company, Tesla Motors, the advanced electric car company, and Space X, the space transport company whose Dragon space craft now supplies the International Space Station in place of the U.S. Space Shuttles. He is also the person whom Jon Favreau, the director of the Iron Man movies, says the character Tony Stark is based on, and Musk had a cameo appearance in those movies. Unfortunately, also reported in the news have been the personal life challenges of Mr. Musk, including the high-profile divorces: one from his first wife, a fiction novelist, who publicly spoke and blogged about their lives and divorce; then recently his divorce from a British actress from whom he split after a year of marriage publicly stating he could not give her what she wants. He has reportedly been described as a workaholic who has been known to put in 100-hour work weeks and who has said he regrets the days where he'd sleep under his desk and obsess about work. Obsession with entrepreneurial endeavors can make it challenging in personal life relationships. But how does the busy entrepreneur make time for his or her family? Over the years, I've come up with a few rules I learned and try to stick to in order to make sure I'm getting as much quality time as I can with my family. Some of my personal rules are as follows:

o **The kids' major events always take precedence—** I always clear the calendar whenever my kids have what I would consider to be a major event. For example, graduating kindergarten might not seem like a big deal to you, but it really is a big deal for your child and for the family, so I always make the effort to be around for events such as these.

o **Do make-ups for my wife and family whenever possible—**I've had to work late nights and on the weekends many times, but I've also made sure that I found ways to do "make-ups" for my family over time. I might take off early one afternoon to go down to the beach with my wife, for example. These "make-ups" never truly repay all the time I've had to be away working, but it's an honest effort to make sure my relationships stay strong. Your family relationships are simply too important to damage.

o **Only travel when needed**—Back when I was a single man, I was constantly traveling for business, but when I got married again I soon realized just how much my traveling would wear on my wife. You can't have strong relationships when you're on the road hundreds of days a year. So, now I only travel when it's absolutely necessary for business. I take advantage of all the technology that's out there for me to connect with customers, vendors, and other people around the world without leaving home.

These are just some of my personal rules. As you grow your business and try to find ways to make time for your family, you can create and evolve some of your own guidelines that will work with your unique family dynamic. Now, does this mean that you'll never be able to stay at work late to complete important tasks or that you can't put in the extra effort by working a weekend here and there to get your business up and running? Of course not. But the point is that you should strive to not lose sight of the importance of your family relationships. You don't want to lose these while building your business.

• **Don't neglect family duties**—This goes hand-in-hand with the last point. There is a very thin line for entrepreneurs between building a business and neglecting your family duties. In addition to making time to spend with your family, you need to make sure you're actually taking care of your responsibilities to the family as well. This might mean checking some items off the "Honey do" list, attending your children's special events (e.g. choir recitals, sports games, etc.), dealing with your children when they get out of line, supporting your partner emotionally, and so on. In other words, it's not enough just to be around from time to time. You need to really be there when you're there. You have to be present, and you have to take care of your family obligations. If you don't, your family will think your business is more important to you than they are, and that's never a good spot to be in.

- **Find trade-offs**—Getting your family's support may require some give and take. What are you willing to do in order to get their support? What trade-offs can you make so that everyone is happy? For example, if you have to spend an entire weekend working and not being with your family, you should try to find a trade-off so that you can make it up to them. Maybe you take a long weekend the following weekend and go on a little trip with them. Or if you're working lots of long hours, maybe you set aside a specific night of the week each week where you'll watch the kids while your spouse gets to go out with some friends. It's all about finding little trade-offs and compromises so you can keep the peace, get your work done, and earn the support of your family.

- **Consider ways they can get involved in your business**—Looking for a way to get your family on board with your business? How about you literally get them on board with your business? Give them something to do so that they're working for your business and it becomes a passion of theirs, too. That's what Noha Waibsnaider, founder of Peeled Snacks, did—she hired her husband to work for her. In the early days of starting up her snacks business, her husband was greatly concerned about her spending the family's life savings on a business that sold dried fruit snacks. Her husband was frightened, but at the same time, he enjoyed seeing the business develop and flourish. So, Noha decided to bring her husband on board as an employee—yes she is his boss, not a co-owner—so he could contribute to the business and have a vested interest in its success. Joanna Meiseles, who is founder of Snip-its, a children's hair care franchise, actually involves her children in the business, getting them to provide their opinions on the company's various products and the videos they produce. Talk about a family business! Is there any way you can get your family involved in your business? Doing so might prove to be a great way to get their support and to eliminate the pressure from them to get a steady, traditional job. The more involved they are in the business, the less critical they might be. Just make sure to draw clear lines in the business. If they're working for you, that has to be clear. You have to clearly define their roles, and at the end of the day, you have to let them know you're still the boss.

## A Successful Business Won't Save Your Relationships

You might think that family relationships will only be difficult to manage when your business is struggling, and while it's true that the added burden of financial problems can compound these issues, the fact is that it's tough to manage family relationships even when your business is prosperous. There is always work to be done, and if you don't make the time for your family, it won't matter how much money you're making, the relationships will still suffer.

Likewise, if you're in a troubled relationship and you think that starting a business and getting it to make money is going to save your relationship, you're barking up the wrong tree. You can't throw money at a broken relationship and make it whole. That's just not how it works. You can't buy a happy, healthy relationship.

In a case such as this, it's important that you really get down to the core of the problems with your relationship. Put the business issues aside for a moment, and focus on what isn't working between you and your spouse or significant other. Your problems won't go away just because your business makes a lot of money. That might help cover them up temporarily, but it won't solve them.

## Examine Your Relationships

I am in no way trying to provide expert marital or relationship advice. However, what I am encouraging is to truly take an honest assessment of one's relationships to make sure that they are healthy and not a barrier to your progress and success as an entrepreneur. You can use all of the tactics I mention and more to provide some stop-gap solutions, but if one has relationships that are unhealthy at their core, these things won't fix it.

In some cases, family pressure and lack of support comes from deeper underlying causes. Not getting support for your entrepreneurial efforts could be a sign of the other bad parts of your relationship. After all, if someone isn't supporting your dreams and passions, are they really supporting *you* as a person? I tend to believe they aren't.

I believe that the right partner is someone who supports you, not someone who brings you down. It's someone who assists you, not someone who resists you. It's someone who motivates you, not someone who criticizes you.

I have heard before that the divorce rate among entrepreneurs is higher than average, although I haven't seen any stats to support this. But if it's true, it doesn't surprise me. It's nearly impossible to build a successful business without the love and support of your spouse and the rest of your immediate family. An unsupportive spouse will kill your resolve, crush your dreams, and eventually force you to choose between them and your business (your dream). The same could be said depending on the situation of unsupportive relatives and friends.

A consideration is to truly step back and examine all of the relationships in your life, starting with the most important (your spouse or significant other) and also assessing those with your relatives and friends. One may find that some of these relationships are beneficial and if needed, can be encouraged with some extra attention and effort, but others may not be desired or salvageable as they are toxic and have too much of a negative influence over your life. Never let yourself be brought down by negative people.

### Financial Management: Dealing with Financial Pressures to Keep a Traditional, Steady Job

Your savings are quickly dwindling, your bank account is near zero, your credit cards are close to maxed out, and you don't know exactly when your next check is coming in. Isn't it great being an entrepreneur?

I'm not trying to scare you away from becoming an entrepreneur, but I am trying to give you a dose of potential reality. This is an undesirable situation that many an entrepreneur has found himself or herself in. Starting a business is tough, and it often requires a lot of money up front, so it's very possible that you could find yourself in a serious financial bind at some point.

Earlier in this chapter, I shared with you the story of Robin and John Sauve, the co-founders of Barkley Logistics. This couple found themselves in a tough financial situation during the formative days of their business. They had already taken on $40,000 in credit card debt, but if they wanted to grow their business to the next level, their financial adviser told them they would need to take out another $75,000 line of credit.

Robin dealt with months of troubled nights filled with anxious dreams, but she and her husband worked hard and eventually with the business on track with new contracts and increasing sales decided to take a leap and apply for the new line of credit. You very well could find yourself in a similar situation. It's just part of being an entrepreneur, as the Suave's have learned in growing more accustomed to their entrepreneurial way of life.

Earlier in the book, I explained the Valley of Death concept. The Valley of Death is the point at which an entrepreneur and a business run out of money before the business has a chance to get off the ground and become profitable. This is also the point where most entrepreneurs feel the pressure to get a traditional job, and they often give up on their dreams and go back to the 9-to-5 grind working for someone else.

I'm here to tell you it doesn't have to be that way. Yes, I know the financial pressures to keep a traditional job. I've felt them before, and who knows, I may feel them again at some point in the future. As an entrepreneur, you just never know. That's part of the challenge. The good news is there are several things you can do to ease the financial pressure without giving up on your entrepreneurial endeavors. It's all about finding a way to support yourself—and your family if you have one—financially until your business starts producing the profits you need to be fully supported financially.

We've already spent quite a bit of time in this book discussing many different ways to acquire capital and to expedite your business idea into a profitable venture; you may wish to refer back to that information. Here are some additional ideas that can get you thinking of ways you can be smarter financially so you can see your dream through:

- **Start your business on the side while you continue to work**—If you or your family are worried about the loss of a steady income when you start your business, you could try to start your business on the side while you still continue to work at your regular job. This way, you'll still have your regular income and all of the benefits that are so important to you and your family (e.g. healthcare, 401k, etc.). Of course, starting a business while keeping a regular job is challenging, but with the right approach, you can be successful and eventually turn your sideline business into a full-time gig that lets you leave your old job behind. Here are a few tips to keep in mind when starting your business on the side:

o   Don't let your performance suffer at work. If your side business makes you a bad employee, you could end up losing your job and facing a serious financial nightmare.

o   Choose a business you're passionate about because you're going to be putting in a lot of long hours between your real job and your new business, so you'd better make sure you truly love what you do. Your passion can carry you through the hard times.

o   Get support from your loved ones. It's a lot of work to keep a stable job and to build a business on the side. You need support wherever you can find it, whether it's in the form of having your parents watch the kids a couple of nights a week or having your spouse pitch in on building the business.

o   Schedule specific times to work on your side business. You need to get into some sort of routine. Otherwise, you'll end up neglecting your side business because you're too tired after a long day's work to devote any time to it, or you'll neglect your steady job by letting your side business overlap into your day job's time.

o   Clearly define goals for your side business. You aren't going to build a successful business on the side overnight. Set measured goals that will guide you to making the transition from being a part-time entrepreneur to being a full-time entrepreneur.

• **Live off your savings**—It's very possible that your business won't start to generate enough of a profit to pay you for a couple of years, or more. How are you going to survive without a paycheck until then? If temporarily keeping your job or getting part-time employment isn't possible in your situation, one of the things you can do is to live off your savings until you start earning money. Of course, in order for you to do this, you need to have enough saved up to support yourself and your family. Unfortunately, the average American doesn't have a lot of personal savings. In February 2012, the average personal savings rate for Americans was just 3.7 percent. Not long after the recession began, we had been saving at a rate of more than 8 percent. According to research from Bankrate.com, 49 percent of Americans don't even have enough money saved to cover three months of expenses, and only 25 percent have enough saved to cover six months of expenses. So, there's a good chance that as you're reading this you might not have enough in savings to quit your job, start your business, and live completely off your savings. In that case, I suggest you get to work immediately to bolster your savings, and in the meantime, perhaps you can utilize some of the other tactics I mention to alleviate financial pressures while starting your business.

- **Be willing to cut back on personal luxuries**—How bad do you really want to start your business? And how bad do you want to avoid having to keep a traditional job? If you want it badly enough, you'll find a way to make ends meet. Oftentimes, that will mean eliminating luxuries and/or making sacrifices. Take a complete inventory of your expenses. Where exactly is your money going right now? And what can you do without? Can you sell the boat or sports car? Do you really need cable TV or that many smartphones? How about your very nice car...could you make do with an older, less expensive one? I'm willing to bet there are possibly different expenses you could cut right now that would save money and help ease some of your financial burden while you work to get your business off the ground. Nobody said this was going to be easy. You'll probably have to make some sacrifices, but if you stick with it and see things through, the payoff could be more than worth it.

- **Keep startup costs as low as possible**—A lot of your expenses will come in the formative days of your business. Turning your idea into an actual business usually costs money, but the good news is that we live in a day and age where there are more options than ever before for keeping your startup costs low. Thanks to the Internet, you can stay connected to your workers and customers easily, eliminating the need for buying or leasing an office in many situations. Another way to keep your costs down is to use freelancers and independent contractors instead of hiring full-time employees. You don't have to pay benefits and employment taxes if you use contractors, so this can save your business a lot of money. The Internet makes it very easy to find reliable, affordable labor to complete all sorts of tasks, from your marketing to your accounting. You could even work with interns, creating a win-win situation for both of you. This gives you the help you need to build your business while also giving interns valuable experience and college credits. Many entrepreneurs have found bartering to be an effective means for keeping their costs down. You may be able to trade your products and services with others for things such as advertising, web design, videos, and more. There are literally dozens of other tactics you can take advantage of to get your business up and running while spending as little money as possible. Again, this is a subject I've explored throughout this book, so you should have the tools you need to get in a creative mindset that allows you to find ways to minimize your startup costs so you can alleviate your financial pressures when building your business.

**Dealing with Pressure**

As an entrepreneur, you're almost always dealing with some sort of pressure. Whether it's the pressures we discussed in this chapter or some other sort of pressure, you need to learn how to manage the pressure, frustration, and anxiety so you can get through it and still get the job done right.

One of the first things you need to do is to learn how to recognize the signs and symptoms that you're under too much pressure. Pressure can cause serious stress on you physically and emotionally, leading to such problems as insomnia, fatigue, stomach problems, headaches, increased use of alcohol, loss of sex drive, anxiety, lack of focus or motivation, overeating, social withdrawal and sadness.

If you're experiencing any of these symptoms, it could be a sign that you're under a lot of pressure at work. Rather than ignoring these symptoms, focus on finding ways to manage the pressure.

Over the years, I've found a number of different methods that have helped me successfully deal with the pressures of running a business. I've learned that it's helpful to:

- **Take a break**—Some days you have to break the tension by getting away from work and doing something else for a bit. There comes a point in the day where you've been working for too long and too hard to be productive anymore, so you just need to step away for a bit so you can come back to work feeling fresh and motivated. A break might mean getting away for an hour to have a meal with someone whose company you enjoy and talk about something else other than work.

- **Slip in mini-escapes**—Sometimes what I call a mini-escape can make a difference in stress levels. This is a time of engaging the senses and thus the mind in something entirely different that frees you from work. It can be as short as some minutes of watching a video of peaceful nature, listening to classical music, or longer as taking a half-day off to be with your family or friends doing an activity that recharges your batteries. Anything that brings you enjoyment taking your mind from the stress and reinvigorates you.

- **Be Active**—Regular exercise provides tremendous benefits in managing pressures encountered as an entrepreneur. Whatever the activity you are motivated to do, the gym, biking, jogging, tennis, swimming, etc., that you will do for 30 minutes or more on a regular basis, will not only increase your heart rate, blood flow and breathing, but also increase your energy, focus and productivity.

- **Take control**—At times issues you're dealing with or what you have to do in a day can seem huge and insurmountable, but every problem and day has a path forward. It's just hard to come up with that solution when you're trying to tackle the whole thing at once. You should try to simplify things by breaking it into its parts and prioritize in order of importance. You will begin to feel more in control, especially as you deliberately plan steps to work through the issue in a way you can manage and as you see progress completing step by step.

- **Take care of yourself**—Your body needs sleep. When you get enough rest, your mind is sharp, your emotions are better balanced, and you're physically healthier as well. I know there is always work to be done, but you really must do your best to aim for an appropriate sleep each night. Lack of sleep will only exacerbate the symptoms of stress. Food choices are important as well, this is your fuel. Eating healthy balanced meals in appropriate portions can help you keep your energy levels up and to stay focused. It's amazing how much better you can feel about things and make progress after good sleep and a healthy meal.

- **Maintain a positive attitude**—Think about good outcomes, be realistic and careful, but avoid negativity and concentrate on the positive. If something is worrying you, deliberately make out a plan for it so you feel that you've addressed it. Be careful of your self-talk going on in your mind so that it is positive about yourself and around things working out well. Then usually they will. As the American Industrialist Henry Ford said, "Whether you think you can or you can't, you're right." Nothing is more self-defeating than negativity; it will steal energy, happiness and success. Lastly, don't short yourself on laughter. As Milton Berle, the comedian and actor said, "Laughter is an instant vacation."

- **Connect with people who understand**—As I said earlier, one of the reasons your family might not support you is because they might not really "get" business and entrepreneurship. Simply put, they might not understand your dream or see why it's so important to you. And in some cases, you won't ever be able to make that totally clear to them. That's why finding support wherever you can get it is important. If your family isn't actively supporting and encouraging you, try to connect with people who better understand where you're coming from. Network with fellow entrepreneurs, or turn to your friends who have a better understanding of business and who are more supportive of your efforts. There are many ways you can find friends who will support you as an entrepreneur. You can attend live events, like conferences and local networking groups, or you can even make friends online, through social media sites like Twitter and Facebook or on forums devoted to entrepreneurs.

- **Take advantage of outside help**—I don't care if this is your first time starting a business or you're a serial entrepreneur, entrepreneurial pressures can wear you down and be too much for you to handle on your own. That's why it's often a smart idea to get outside help and coaching from a professional business advisor. This can bring fresh perspectives, analysis and ideas. Talking to someone who is not a family member or friend and is an unbiased professional can make a significant positive difference. With a seasoned advisor by your side, you can get the steady hand and encouragement you need. Yes, it costs some money to hire a business coach, but think of it as an investment that returns value. An experienced and knowledgeable advisor in your corner can help you cross this very important entrepreneurial barrier so you can see your business idea all the way through.

## Pursuit of Happiness

As an entrepreneur you're not always going to have just good times. There will be ups and downs, good times and bad times. There will be periods where you're discouraged. But what will keep you going? Passion.

What is it? An intense driving desire that has the word love as a synonym, and that burning desire or love for something is what enables a person to put forth any effort and bear any pressure. It's what makes working from 7 a.m. to 11 p.m. to fly by and without feeling tired. Entrepreneurs are individuals who are passionate about their endeavor and that passion drives them onward so they can make their dreams a reality. If you're truly passionate about your business dream you can find a way over barriers and achieve a bridge to your goals of success.

The questions for each individual to answer is do you love what you're doing, are you passionate about it? Unfortunately, too many times, people are caught up in the rat race of a monotonous running of their life and careers that is void of passion and seemingly pointless without an opportunity of an end game where they reap satisfying rewards. They are not attempting the fulfillment of their ambitions and better useful purpose. Theodore Roosevelt, 26th President of the United States summed it up well, "Far better it is to dare mighty things, to win glorious triumphs, even though checkered by failure, than to take rank with those poor spirits who neither enjoy much nor suffer much because they live in the gray twilight that knows neither victory nor defeat."

The Founding Fathers of the United States of America understood entrepreneurialism. There were successful entrepreneurs among them, such as Benjamin Franklin the inventor, who was the first famous American entrepreneur. This understanding is also very obvious in the document they drafted, named the Declaration of Independence which was primarily drafted by Thomas Jefferson and adopted by the Second Continental Congress on July 4, 1776. The words of the second section of the Declaration are quoted down below.

In the liberty of your life, are you pursuing what makes you happy?

"We hold these truths to be self-evident, that all men are created equal, that they are endowed by their Creator with certain unalienable Rights, that among these are Life, Liberty and the pursuit of Happiness"

~ Founding Fathers, United States of America

# 11

## CHARACTERISTICS OF AN ENTREPRENEUR

As you have read through this book and discovered some of the barriers that loom large throughout the entrepreneurial journey, you might be asking yourself, "What kind of person is equipped to handle these challenges? The reality is not all of us are bridge builders. Starting your own business is tough, and many wannabe entrepreneurs do not realize their dreams.

A goal of this book has been to share information not only about the challenges but also the methods and attitudes to assist you in becoming a successful entrepreneur. While you've started to learn some of the strategies for building bridges over the most common barriers you may face as you start a business, it's also important that you learn and understand the behaviors and characteristics that drive successful entrepreneurs. When you understand what makes others successful, you can better position yourself for success.

So, just what lies at the core of a successful entrepreneur? What are some of the characteristics the most successful entrepreneurs share? What does the ideal entrepreneur look like? Throughout this chapter, we'll address such questions with the goal of providing useful insights and observations into what makes an entrepreneur successful.

## The Myths

The ancient Greeks told stories about their pantheon of gods and goddesses who were heroes living on Mount Olympus, which we know were myths to help them explain the occurrence of events in life. With all the stories and comparisons told these days about entrepreneurs one could think that they are rare, special geniuses that were born heroes which explains why they are unlike the rest of us. No, entrepreneurs are not all like Richard Branson, Mark Cuban, Steve Jobs, Elon Musk, or Bill Gates. In fact, there are many myths held in the general perceptions about entrepreneurs. Let's look at a couple of important myths:

- **Entrepreneurs are rare and unique**—So, what does the typical successful entrepreneur look like? When describing someone, it makes sense to begin with their physical appearance. Are entrepreneurs male or female? Young or old? Caucasian, African American, Asian, or Hispanic? As you could probably guess, entrepreneurs come in all shapes and sizes. There are successful male and female entrepreneurs, young and old entrepreneurs, and entrepreneurs of every race. It's a myth they are rare. Let's take a closer look at some statistics that show just how common and diverse the entrepreneurial landscape is:

o   **Entrepreneurs come from all over**—According to
    the Global Entrepreneurship Monitor (GEM), about
    330 million people around the world (14 percent of
    the adults in the 35 countries surveyed) are involved
    in forming new businesses.

o   **Women-owned businesses are on the rise**—In
    2002, there were 6.5 million women-owned
    businesses. This represented a 20 percent increase
    from 1997. In 2007, the number of women-owned
    businesses was closer to 8 million.

o   **Minority-owned businesses see significant
    increase**—According to the U.S. Census Bureau,
    minority-owned businesses increased 45.5 percent
    from 2002 to 2007 from 4 million businesses to 5.8
    million businesses. These businesses accounted for
    21.3 percent of the nation's businesses, employed
    5.8 million people, and generated $1 trillion in
    receipts.

o   **Age is nothing but a number**—It's never too early
    or too late to start a business. While you might think
    entrepreneurship is a young person's game, the truth
    is that a recent Kauffman survey, "The Anatomy of
    an Entrepreneur", found that the average and median
    age of company founders when they started their
    current companies was 40. Some have argued that
    the peak age for today's internet entrepreneur is 25,
    but the truth is that the number of self-employed
    people ages 55 to 64 is increasing rapidly, climbing
    52 percent from 2000 to 2007, according to the
    Small Business Administration. In other words,

entrepreneurs can be young or old; it doesn't matter. In fact, a recent study from the Kauffman Foundation revealed that the highest rate of entrepreneurship in America has shifted to the 55-64 age group. People over the age of 55 are almost twice as likely to found successful companies than those between the ages of 20 and 34. It's never too late to chase the dream.

o **Outsiders can make for great entrepreneurs too**—In a 2007 Quick Books survey of 1,300 small business owners with 20 or fewer employees, 43 percent of entrepreneurs say they were "loners" as kids, while 25 percent said they would have been described as "nerds." In other words, about half of the entrepreneurs surveyed could be described as outsiders. They were people who didn't really fit in. They weren't the popular kids in school. They probably didn't wear the right clothes, drive the right car, or take part in the right afterschool activities. Just think of some of the most successful entrepreneurs of our lifetime—Bill Gates and Steve Jobs are perfect examples of people who didn't quite fit in when building their own entrepreneurial bridges in the world. Mark Rice, Dean of the Graduate School of Business at Babson College told Fox News that "people who have the personality and motivation to be the leader and start something on their own are more inclined to feel like they aren't part of the social structure. Entrepreneurs by definition are different. They are doing something on the fringe."

- **Entrepreneurs are born, not made**—Entrepreneurship isn't something you're born into. It doesn't run in your family's genes. Just because your parents weren't entrepreneurs doesn't mean that you don't have what it takes to be a successful business owner and vice versa. No, entrepreneurs are made. It's a myth they are only born. They are made by their experiences, education, and training. Sure, some do share certain inborn characteristics, like the willingness to take risks and openness to changing, but the fact remains that entrepreneurs are made. Here are some statistics that support this assertion:

  o **Transition to Entrepreneur**—More than half of all entrepreneurs surveyed by Ernst & Young in *Nature or Nurture? Decoding the DNA of the Entrepreneur* described themselves as "transitioned" entrepreneurs. In other words, they had spent time gaining valuable experience and training from a traditional job before starting their own venture.

  o **Work experience important factor**—When asked to rank the factors that contributed to their business' success in order of importance, the entrepreneurs surveyed by Ernst & Young were most likely to select "experience as an employee" as the most important factor influencing their success. More simply stated, their job groomed them for success as an entrepreneur. Also, according to a Harvard Business School paper entitled *Performance Persistence in Entrepreneurship*, "a substantial fraction of the Inc. 500 got their idea for their new company while working at their prior employer."

o **Various success factors found**—Some other success factors ranked number one by the entrepreneurs in the Ernst & Young survey included higher education (30 percent), mentors (26 percent), family (21 percent), and secondary education (13 percent). Again, these entrepreneurs were describing themselves as being made, not born.

I think you get the point. Successful entrepreneurs are a product of their experiences, education and training. They use the skills and resources they develop through their education, traditional job, and networking to help launch their ventures.

That's why I always encourage those thinking about starting a business to take a close look at their experience, skills, resources, and connections. Your best chance of success comes when you put these assets to work for you. If you've received training and employment in the tech industry, you'll probably have a greater chance of success launching a tech startup than a restaurant.

Sticking with what you know and are familiar with is a key to positioning yourself for success. The further you stray from your experience, skills, resources, and connections, the likelier it becomes that you'll fail.

**The Right Stuff**

So what does it take to be a successful entrepreneur? It's a fair question. The truth is that not everyone is right for entrepreneurship.

"The Right Stuff" is the title of a famous 1983 American film adapted from the 1979 book written by Tom Wolfe of the same title. It's about the military test pilots at Edwards Air Force Base who flew high-speed experimental aircraft and were the group chosen by NASA to select the astronauts from for manning the flights into outer space.

Several groups were considered, such as aviators, polar explorers, mountain climbers, and others that had demonstrated abilities for dangerous new adventures. But the military test pilots were chosen when it was determined they had "the right stuff," or the right combination of characteristics in areas as training, experience, skills, personality, physical and mental traits for the space program. And rightly so, it was a dangerous and risky effort to venture into space for the first time and then travel to the Earth's moon.

NASA put the applicants from this group through a rigorous review and selection process. The selection process included the severe physical testing that became famous, but also personal characteristics inventory testing looking at traits such as goal seeking, achievement motivation, emotional stability, work orientation, mastery, and interpersonal sensitivity. They looked for an overall profile with behaviors such as: ability to tolerate high risk and stress situations while maintaining problem-solving logical thought; leadership with decision making while in states of high mental and physical endurance; taking personal responsibility but also working well with others.

NASA needed individuals with a profile that came to be known as "the right stuff," with the combination of traits that predicted high performance in confined and hazardous settings as spaceflight. It was only those that passed the final stage astronaut selection, such as Alan Shepard and John Glenn of the Mercury Seven in the first space flights, and Neil Armstrong, of the Gemini and Apollo programs, who was the first man to walk on the moon, that would be allowed the chance to venture into space and bravely go where no man had gone before.

Now I'm not saying that entrepreneurs need to have the same characteristics as astronauts or should be comparable to them. But I do think there are parallels that can be drawn from this. Just as there were characteristics that indicated the performance of successful astronauts, likewise there are characteristics that are the right stuff for individuals to be more successful as an entrepreneur. Entrepreneurs work in challenging business environments where they must cope with significant risk and stress, and need characteristics such as appropriate training, experience and skills that provide qualities that can support a business venture.

## The Research

Not only did my entrepreneurial research lead me to reading NASA research papers on the psychology of space exploration, but also to reviewing research and studies of entrepreneur competency that has been done around the world including the Americas, Europe and Asia. These included various university and government studies, and also fundamental and influential works of authors the likes of D.C. McClelland, B. Bird, T.W. Man, G.N. Chandler, and many others on entrepreneur competency. Why I appreciate this research is it not only includes the observations and thoughts of scholars, which is to be respected and considered, but more importantly includes feedback data from actual entrepreneurs providing empirical validation to conclusions.

Found in these entrepreneurial researches are descriptions of competencies in a model for entrepreneurs. A competency model can clearly define the skills, knowledge, attitudes and behaviors which the individual needs to perform the role. These help in better understanding the link between characteristics of entrepreneurs and their business success. The competencies were a way to organize the key characteristics of the entrepreneur into major domains or key areas. In addition, this included defining the competencies in themes or clusters of characteristics including skills, knowledge, attitudes, and behaviors, which are seen as the overall ability of the entrepreneur to perform the role effectively so to achieve business goals successfully. The research also demonstrated that these can be improved via training and development.

**Entrepreneur Competencies**

These is a lot of misinformation out there, and list after list with various numbers of key, essential, required, top, etc., characteristics of an entrepreneur. However, from the research, the following entrepreneurial key competency domains were defined as being fundamentally important for the entrepreneurial journey. With the strength of the entrepreneur's characteristics as key to the degree of success in starting and growing ventures. Here are nine competency areas of entrepreneurs that research reviewed has identified:

- **Strategic**—Developing and implementing vision and strategies for the business

- **Commitment**—Demonstrating strong motivations and drive to move the business ahead

- **Conceptual**—Cognitive ability and decision-making skill that demonstrates ability to be creative and innovative while reasoning analytically and weighing the risks; some empirical studies showed entrepreneurs rating this one as most valuable and beneficial

- **Opportunity**—Ability to recognize market situations with conditions favorable to attain the desired goal

- **Organizing and Leading**—Demonstrated by the ability to lead, direct, delegate, motivate, schedule and manage the resources of the business

- **Relationship**—Ability for person-to-person or individual-to-group based interactions building a context of trust and cooperation using connections, persuasion, communication, and interpersonal skill

- **Learning**—Demonstrates ability to proactively gain knowledge or skill by study, experience, or teaching and applying it in actual practice

- **Personal**—Demonstrate high self-motivation and awareness with self-confidence, drive to achieve, resilience, time management, accountability, persistence and determination

- **Technical**—Ability to demonstrate technical skills with tools, procedures, and techniques showing an understanding of business and industry

Now all of these competencies also have utility with the evaluation of individuals as entrepreneurs, especially as it relates to three important states of ability for the individual to each one. First is that of **capability**. This asks what is the current state of an individual's ability in each competency area. Do they currently demonstrate a needed level of capable performance in each one so to function as an entrepreneur?

Secondly is that of **trainability**. No person is a perfect individual who would encompass all these competencies in their full completeness. There are variables of context that influence the ability to perform. Such as what is the current business environment, the condition of the market focused on, the entrepreneurs' background, as well as the degree the selected business idea is the best use of the entrepreneur's capabilities. Everyone has room for improvement whether realized or not. Hence the importance of how trainable the individual is to make up current deficits with learning to increase the performance in needed areas to an acceptable level.

Third is that of **adaptability**. What are the abilities of the individual to adapt? So to be able to process information, make recognitions and adjustments to new conditions in their environments so to enhance their performance ability.

So overall the competency model with its evaluation utility is a useful tool that helps individuals discover, learn and improve their abilities to be a successful entrepreneur. This is why we utilize it in the first phase of the Accelerated Entrepreneur Roadmap system as an important step in a person's entrepreneurial journey. Not as an absolute assessment tool with guaranteed reliability, but as an evaluation method to facilitate the individual to compare themselves to the competencies in the entrepreneur role. In so doing they can learn about the characteristics of entrepreneurs, discover more about their capabilities for the role, and in determining their strengths or weaknesses in each competency they are provided a fit-gap analysis they can use to improve their abilities. It provides the individual awareness and the opportunity to leverage their strengths and improve their weaknesses on their entrepreneurial journey or to determine if it is not a path for them.

## Important Characteristics of Successful Entrepreneurs

I could write an entire book on the intricacies of the successful entrepreneur's characteristics, but rather than try to exhaustively cover here every characteristic these business owners share, let's touch on some important ones for now:

- **They know how to give up control**—While it's true that many become entrepreneurs because they want independence and control, the best entrepreneurs understand that when you own a business you're often faced with the choice: be rich or be in control. A lot goes into running a business, and while you might not mind wearing a lot of hats, the more hats you wear, the less effective you'll be. You must know when it's time to bring in outside talent to help grow your business. Richard Reed of Innocent Drinks understood the importance of handing over control to help grow his business. When he and his two fellow directors sold a stake in their company to Coca-Cola in 2009, they did so to get Coke's help to expand their brand across Europe. Innocent Drinks has had much success by giving up control. They still make healthy fruit drinks, but now they sell much more of them. Of course, entrepreneurs are often a stubborn bunch, resistant to asking for help. But the truth is you just can't do it all yourself. You must learn to delegate. To be effective at delegating, you should:

  - Delegate the tasks that are either outside of your expertise or that could be easily performed by others.

o Create a clear process for completing the task that you're delegating, so the person you've hired will do it properly.

o Hire the right talent to handle the tasks at hand. This means understanding which skill sets are needed to complete the task.

o Set measurable goals and hold employees accountable for their performance.

o Check in on the employee's progress regularly, but resist the urge to micromanage.

- **They learn from others**—The smart entrepreneur realizes that he doesn't know it all. He knows that knowledge is power, and he understands that the more he learns, the better his chances are of success. Successful entrepreneurs get educated in a number of ways—through institutions, peers, business advisors, books…you name it. Learning is a lifelong process. If you want to be a successful entrepreneur, you must be a lifelong learner. You should glean knowledge at all times and in all places.

- **They are effective networkers**—You've heard people say, "it's not what you know, it's who you know." There is certainly some truth to this. Entrepreneurs are well-advised to build strong networks of resources so they can get the support they need to succeed. Having a strong network of connections can help you with raising capital, hiring employees, finding vendors, generating new leads, and continuing your learning. I strongly recommend focusing your efforts on expanding your network. There are many different ways to do this, from social networking like Facebook, Twitter and LinkedIn to attending business networking events in your town.

- **They have values**—According to the report published by Ernst & Young, "entrepreneurial leaders typically have a strong, consistent set of values that drives their overall behavior in their professional lives." Strength of character is important to entrepreneurial success. These values drive every key decision the entrepreneur makes, and they are often used to create a unique company culture. Furthermore, successful entrepreneurs seek out people that share their values. When hiring employees, they place a premium on finding talented individuals who share their values, whether it be a strong work ethic, integrity, or passion for the industry.

- **They have the desire to be successful**—You can typically assess an individual's potential for entrepreneurial success by determining whether or not they possess that burning seed of desire deep down inside of them. When legendary NBA coach Phil Jackson gets asked what made Michael Jordan such a remarkable player, he often answers by saying it was his undying will to win. Successful entrepreneurs have that same will to win. They have heart and determination, and they refuse to let any obstacle stand in their way. Look deep inside yourself. How bad do you really want it? What are you willing to do to be successful? Are you truly willing to put in the time and effort it takes to get your business to where you want it to be?

- **They see opportunity in disruption**—Entrepreneurs tend to be perennial optimists. Perhaps that's one of the explanations for why entrepreneurship has a history of increasing during tough economic times. When others cower in fear of a bad economy, the optimistic entrepreneur sees opportunities and believes they can find a way to capitalize on them. I truly believe that being an optimist is essential for entrepreneurial success. However, I encourage you to always temper your optimism with realism so that you don't take unwise risks. Over-optimism can set you up for failure in the form of unrealistic sales projections, inaccurate cash flow projections, incorrect start-up capital estimations, and a host of other ways.

- **They take action rather than wait for good things to happen**—Successful entrepreneurs often share a belief that for positive events to take place they must first take the right actions. In other words, entrepreneurial leaders take ownership of situations and they take action. They don't sit on their hands and wait for something good to happen. They are proactive and they make things happen. You have to realize that you have control over your environment. Anything you want to achieve, you have the power to do it. All you have to do is take control of the situation and take action.

- **They have a high tolerance for risk-taking and failure**—By now, you know that the lack of willingness to take risks is the biggest deterrent to becoming an entrepreneur. Those that do take the leap have a high tolerance for risk-taking and failure. They understand they could very well fail spectacularly, but they also firmly believe that the potential rewards for success make the risk well worth it. In fact, many entrepreneurs view failure as a badge of honor. They may get knocked down, but you can be sure that the true entrepreneur will get back up, dust themselves off, learn from their mistakes, and give it another shot. They take it on the chin, get up, and do it again. Caterina Fake, co-founder of Flickr (the online image and video sharing community), went two years without being paid for her work in starting the company. She mortgaged her house to put money back into the company, risking her personal and professional well-being. The risk paid off in spades. In 2005, Yahoo! bought Flickr for an amount rumored to be around $35 million. I highly recommend taking a close, honest look at your level of risk tolerance. If risk and fear of failure paralyzes you, maybe starting your own business isn't the wisest course of action.

- **They are persistent**—You've probably heard the old saying, "a smooth sea never made a skillful mariner." That certainly applies to being an entrepreneur. Sure, there are those rare cases where a first-time entrepreneur has everything go his way and his venture turns into a billion dollar enterprise, but that's the exception, not the rule. Typically, entrepreneurs face major struggles when launching a business. Heck, that's what this whole book is about—the barriers you'll face along your entrepreneurial journey. What separates the successful entrepreneur from the wannabe entrepreneur is persistence. Successful entrepreneurs don't give up when times get tough. They don't throw in the towel at the first sign of trouble. Instead, the successful entrepreneur adapts. They build bridges over any barrier that presents itself. They perform well under pressure, and address each challenge with confidence and perseverance. Let's not forget that history is replete with examples of entrepreneurs who overcame countless failures before achieving remarkable success. Milton Hershey endured years of failure before finally becoming the king of candy. Thomas Edison persevered through more than 10,000 failed experiments before finally getting his light bulb to work (Edison was quoted as saying, "I have not failed. I've just found 10,000 ways that won't work."). Walt Disney's company was $4 million in debt in the early 1930s before turning things around with the blockbuster movie *Snow White and the Seven Dwarfs*.

They never give up.

- **They have the intangibles**—Successful entrepreneurs often have intangible assets that aid them in achieving their goals. A closer look at the responses from successful entrepreneurs in both the Ernst & Young and Kauffman studies finds that some of the most commonly cited intangible characteristics of entrepreneurs include:

o   Creativity

o   Innovation

o   Passion

o   Faith

o   Optimism

o   Timing

## Is There an Entrepreneur in You?

You now have a clearer picture of the successful entrepreneur, and you may be wondering if you have an entrepreneur in you. Do you really have what it takes to be a successful business owner and build bridges over the challenges?

I've developed an online self-assessment questionnaire to help people determine if they are the entrepreneurial type. I invite you to take this self-assessment questionnaire absolutely free on my website www.successfulentrepreneuradvisor.com.

After you complete the questionnaire, a report will be composed based on your answers and sent directly to your email, so you can have the beginning of your own discovery about the journey of the entrepreneur.

# 12

## CONCLUSION — ENTREPRENEUR BRIDGE TO THE AMERICAN DREAM

On any trip you might take, you would not go far if you did not have bridges to cross the barriers as rivers and ravines that would be encountered. It took someone with knowledge, skill, persistence and hard work to build the bridges that overcome such barriers so that travel can be successful to a destination.

In reading this book, you have went on a journey in which you encountered the seven top barriers for entrepreneurs and have learned of attitudes and approaches to help you build bridges over barriers as you continue your entrepreneurial journey to business success. Now you are more of an entrepreneurial bridge builder, with awareness of barriers and their challenges but also understanding how you can better prepare to bridge over them to your business dreams.

## Follow Bridge Building Basics for Entrepreneurial Success

When the right components and methods are used to build bridges they can withstand the forces they must and consistently support the loads they bear, if they are not, then it ultimately leads to disasters. One such bridge disaster well-known to engineers is that of the Tacoma Narrows Bridge in the state of Washington, a spectacular failure on November 7, 1940, caught on film. Technically the cause of collapse was aeroelastic flutter, which basically was a torqueing vibration of the bridge from high wind until it collapsed. However, it is known that financing for the bridge was a problem from the beginning, resulting in adjustments to the design to reduce cost but also caused it to be made weaker. The dramatic collapse is still used in engineering classes and textbooks as a case study failure.

Just as it's necessary for engineers to have an understanding of the properties of various building materials and of construction methods for building bridges so they can appropriately withstand external forces and loads, span barriers and distances, and do so at a reasonable cost, so must the entrepreneur be a bridge builder to overcome barriers in your entrepreneurial path to your destination of success. In this book, you have found statistics, advice, methods, and entrepreneurial stories that will help you develop the entrepreneur bridge mentality to overcoming obstacles you will face. How well you can build bridges to get over the barriers you encounter when starting and building a business will determine your entrepreneurial success. Here are a few final bridge building basics to consider:

- **Learn from master builders**—It's important that novice engineers after their studies learn from master builders who have the experience in overseeing projects and using right methods and materials to build expensive structures over serious hazards with significant risk to life. Likewise, to learn from the real world experience of successful entrepreneurs provides the opportunity for aspiring and improving entrepreneurs to learn from those who have successfully bridged barriers to success. Take every opportunity to learn from their stories and follow those examples which helps individuals discover what is necessary, avoid mistakes and speed their own path to success.

- **Use the best bridge-building practices**—When engineers build a bridge they make sure to use the best materials and methods suitable for the situation to ensure its strength and safety. They dig down to bedrock for a solid and anchored foundation, use proper geometrical structured material designed to withstand external forces and internal pressures, and make it short as possible all the while using strong connections. As an entrepreneur, you always will want to seek and learn to use the best ways in starting and building your business, making sure to develop strong connections with mentors and customers, finding the shortest path to cash flow, all the while managing wisely the pressures and stresses of the time and effort required in building the strong foundation of a successful business.

- **Use accelerated construction techniques to save time and cost**—From the many years of experience and innovation in building many successful bridges for various situations and requirements, bridge building has evolved and progressed. Now engineers take advantage of this accumulated knowledge and leverage it in a collection of methods and tools that can shave months, potentially years, from the time required to build a bridge. With advanced materials, smart sensing technology and life cycle management techniques, these accelerated construction methods result in quality successful bridge projects with huge savings of time and cost. Likewise, today's entrepreneur can wisely take advantage of the Accelerated Entrepreneur Roadmap shared in this book, available to them from years of accumulated business research and experience. A rapid, systematic roadmap providing approaches and methods the average person can use to help more rapidly start and improve their business, in less time and cost while helping reduce the risk of failure.

- **Don't listen to the naysayers**—Whether it was the Roebling Family building the Brooklyn Bridge or Joseph Strauss building the Golden Gate Bridge, they always had people around telling them that it couldn't be done. They faced opposition from all angles. But what did they do? They tuned them out, and went to work to pursue their vision. As an entrepreneur, you'll probably have to deal with some naysayers along the way. Whether it's a family member pressuring you to get a real job, an employee questioning your leadership capabilities or a competitor threatening to squash you, the negative noise will sometimes surround you. Don't give in to it. If you have a clear vision, pursue it and reach for your dreams.

- **Always be innovating**—Not only were they bridge builders but it was also necessary for those engineers as Roebling and Strauss to be innovators. Their innovations allowed for a better bridge and a safer workplace. As an entrepreneur, you should be a prolific innovator. Don't get stuck doing things like everyone else or believing that something can't be done. When you face a challenge that seems impossible to overcome, don't give up—create the solution. Be the innovator. The entrepreneurs with the characteristic of innovation are the ones who reach that level of success that all others aspire to.

- **Persistence is key**—The builders of great bridges did not see their vision fulfilled overnight. As previously described it took the Roebling family fourteen years to build the Brooklyn Bridge. It took Joseph Strauss and his team over four years to build the Golden Gate Bridge, but he first had his idea for it back in the 1920s. Construction on the bridge didn't begin until 1933, and it wasn't completed until 1937. Along the way, they faced a number of barriers, but they never gave up on their dream. They saw it through and achieved things no other bridge-builder before them had ever done. As an entrepreneur, you must show this same level of persistence. Just because you have a great business idea doesn't mean that you're going to be successful immediately. You're going to have to put in a lot of hard work, and along the way, you're going to be met with a number of barriers that will test your very mettle. But the intrepid entrepreneur will face every challenge with great resolve, and that entrepreneur will keep working until he or she builds enough bridges over their barriers to achieve his or her dreams.

- **You have to take risky endeavors if you want to achieve your dream**—Building the Brooklyn Bridge or the Golden Gate Bridge in their day was a huge gamble. In that time building such bridges seemed nearly impossible. The builders had to overcome such huge physical barriers and build bridges of such strength and distance as had never been done before at that time. The builders knew it was risky and that the odds could be against them, but they managed the risks and with new methods developed bridges that would become landmarks of history. As you probably remember, one of the biggest barriers facing entrepreneurs is the unwillingness to take risks. If you want to be an entrepreneur, you have to be willing to take risks, that's all there is to it. You can't start your own business without taking risks. But if you can learn to manage the risks and have a clear vision and roadmap for what you want to achieve, it can be a thrilling, albeit life changing, journey as you strive to turn your business idea into a reality.

## The Entrepreneur Bridge to the American Dream

In the year 2012, the same year that I wrote this book, the 75th anniversary of the Golden Gate Bridge was celebrated. It is not just a bridge over the Golden Gate Strait of the entrance to the San Francisco Bay from the Pacific Ocean, but it is an iconic landmark that has come to represent so much more.

Before the Golden Gate Bridge was built, the only way across the San Francisco Bay was by ferry. In the 1920's, the Bay was clogged with ferries, and it was recognized that a bridge was needed across the Golden Gate. Many said it couldn't be done, but Joseph Strauss, an engineer and bridge-builder, believed it could.

However, when he proposed the idea, he was met with fierce resistance from a number of groups—the military, loggers, and the railroads. There was also the fact that Strauss would build this bridge during what had become the Great Depression. Needless to say, there wasn't a lot of money floating around to finance this project. So, raising capital was yet another barrier Strauss would have to find a way across. Compounding this was the enormous engineering challenges of building a bridge such a long distance in an area with winds that often reach 60 miles per hour, strong ocean currents that tear through the rugged canyon terrain beneath the surface, and real potential of the pressures and stress of earthquakes.

In short, if Strauss wanted to build the Golden Gate Bridge, he was going to have to overcome a number of barriers. Sure, he could have just given up and nobody would have blamed him. He faced some seemingly insurmountable obstacles. But like all bridge-builders, Strauss was determined to get the job done no matter what it took.

So he went to the people and built support until San Francisco voters approved $35 million in bonds to construct the Golden Gate Bridge. He and his team innovatively designed and built an extended suspension bridge mathematically engineered to overcome the physical barriers. Along the way also setting new standards in construction safety, requiring workers to wear hard hats and take daily sobriety tests – both innovative practices for the era.

The Golden Gate Bridge became an iconic landmark that has come to represent the American dream. The reason it is so iconic goes far beyond its actual physical purpose of getting people across the San Francisco Bay. No, the Golden Gate Bridge represents a dream realized. It represents the hard work and sacrifices necessary to make a dream a reality. To immigrants and people around the world, it is considered a great structure representing overcoming barriers and coming together with freedom, hope and opportunity.

Just as the Golden Gate Bridge encapsulates the American Dream, with the impossible task becoming the possible dream, you can build the entrepreneur bridge to your American Dream of building a business, with the opportunity for the chance of success and freedom.

As you continue to pursue your journey of entrepreneurial dreams, I would like to continue supporting your success, by providing you information, motivation, and methods that help you bridge the barriers to success, as you build your entrepreneur bridge to your dreams. I look forward to you visiting our websites and hearing from you as you continue your entrepreneurial journey.

To Your Success,

W. Glen Thompson

*www.successfulentrepreneuradvisor.com*
*www.acceleratedentrepreneur.com*

# 13

## ABOUT THE AUTHOR — JOURNEY OF ONE ENTREPRENEUR

Every entrepreneur has their own unique story that's filled with twists and turns and highs and lows. I'm no different. This book is the result of my always educational, often unpredictable journey thus far as an entrepreneur. It is a journey, I believe, for most entrepreneurs. It's not a straight line, not one sudden decision, but a path of learning, experiences and then realizations about one's self leading to an entrepreneurial destination. To help you better understand where I'm coming from when I dole out advice or offer up words of inspiration, it only seems logical to briefly share parts of my story with you.

Of course, a lot more things have happened than I can share within these pages, so for the sake of brevity, I must leave certain things out. I share what I do with you, some of it even very personal, in the desire that it's beneficial to you, your goals and dreams. I'm not telling you any of this because I want to brag about how great I am. I'm not great. I'm no better than you or anyone else. And that's the point. I believe people in America have the potential and the opportunity to be successful as an entrepreneur. You can call it the American Dream or whatever else you want to call it, but it's real and it can be yours. You just have to want it.

## My Credentials

Before I get into my real story, you might be asking yourself, "Who is Glen Thompson, and why should I listen to anything he has to say?" Good question. Let me briefly give you some of the bullet points of my career:

- Nearly two decades of successful business consulting experience

- Provided business consulting to customers in the Americas, Europe, and Asia

- Supported entrepreneurs in successfully launching new businesses

- Advised individuals in achieving life goals

- Assisted Fortune 500 companies in transforming their businesses

- Business System Engineer for Electronic Data Systems

- IBM Associate Partner for global business services

- Director for KPMG LLP Advisory Services

- Principal for Andersen Business Consulting

- Business author, speaker and coach

- Founder of my own companies and proprietary methodologies for entrepreneur and business success

Now that I've gotten that out of the way, allow me to take a step back and share my real story with you.

## Humble Beginnings

I grew up, by some people's standards, a poor country boy on a farm in rural Louisiana, but I didn't know it. Even now, I look back on it as an enriching experience. Growing up in a rural setting was wonderful in those days, allowing me the chance to walk the trails in the open countryside free to discover the woods, rivers and lakes while enjoying the scenery and often fishing and hunting. I was very happy, and I still miss it at times, for its sheer joy of simplicity and natural beauty. I also appreciated the values that were instilled in me by family, elders, and the hard work of farm life…values such as integrity, consistency, faith and persistency, to name just a few. I am especially grateful for the teachings of a wonderful, saintly mother who always whispered things in my ear—things like "you can do anything you decide to do," "always believe in yourself and keep the Faith," and "get started now and get it done."

As a young person, I learned how to work hard and do the best you can. I still remember a family meal when we sat down to the dinner table with only bread and gravy to eat and water to drink. It wasn't that my parents didn't care or weren't trying; they were doing the best they could. Although they never graduated from high school (later they got their GED), they got the best jobs they could and worked hard. It just took everybody doing what they could to make it. Make it we did, and I appreciate what my parents taught me and the examples they set for me.

I quickly learned that the only way to get the things I needed and wanted was to get to work and make whatever money I could. I remember wearing worn-out, old blue jeans that had holes in the knees and thin slits, but believe me, it was not because it was in fashion then. When I worked each summer, some of the money I made would go toward buying my school clothes for the next year. When I was getting old enough to drive and wanted to get my own car, I had to work hard to pay for it. My parents signed for me to get my first car, but I was the one who had to make the payments. I was already learning that nothing in life would be handed to me. If I wanted something, I had to work for it. This is something I've never forgotten as an entrepreneur and advisor.

When it came time for me to go to college, I went to a seminary that included theological and historical studies. I had to pay for that, too. I went to class during the day, worked at night (first as a janitor in a junior high school then a grease monkey in a machine shop), and got to sleep on the weekend. One thing I knew: I wanted to make it, whatever make it would be for me, and I did not want to be poor. So I worked hard, studied hard, and stretched myself time and again as I needed to achieve my dreams. To me, there was no alternative. You figure it out, you do it, and you make it. I wasn't looking for someone else to come to the rescue and give me a handout, because there wasn't anybody else. I was making my own way. It was great training for being an entrepreneur!

## My Entrepreneurial Journey

When I decided I wanted to start my first business as an entrepreneur so I could make some money, I looked around at what I had to use and what my opportunities were, which is typical for many entrepreneurs. I was just a kid, so I didn't have much to use. In fact, all I had to use was the family lawnmower, which I was just old enough to push around. The customer landscape was just the people's lawns in our village there in our parish in rural, northeast Louisiana. The good thing was I didn't have much competition at the time, so it looked like I had a niche. I hadn't seen anybody else out hustling to cut our neighbors' yards. Back then, everybody knew each other, and everybody was considered your neighbor, so relationship management was a natural. I asked my folks for permission to use the lawnmower, which was graciously approved (I'm pretty sure they looked at it as a way to keep me busy and out of trouble).

With a functioning lawnmower as my sole business asset, I hit the streets going from house to house asking neighbors if I could mow their yard. I charged $3 for a regular yard and $5 for the larger ones, which I thought was great service pricing. I had a decent reputation in the community, people knew my family, and many of my neighbors thought I was offering them a good deal. So, the business was a success. I made some decent cash in the summers. That's how it all started. Nothing glamorous...just a business born out of financial necessity, finding opportunity, and having a desire to be successful. I've been interested in entrepreneurialism and bettering myself ever since.

In time I moved on as I got older and serviced local grocery stores where I stocked shelves and cleaned up the stores in the evenings after school and on Saturdays. I also knew how to read blueprints because my father was a carpenter. So that helped me to get work also with construction crews building houses while I was in high school. In time, I made enough money to buy my own car, a red Ford Fairlane. I thought that car was hot, and because it was my first ride, it will always have a special place in my heart.

Later on, knowing how to read blueprints proved once again to be a valuable skill set. It got me into operating computerized numerical-controlled machines in manufacturing and then programming them. That was the start eventually leading to me implementing robotic flexible manufacturing systems. I thought all this was cool but knew that there was more opportunity and money to be made in the world than what I had. I had this desire and vision of me sitting in a fine conference room advising in business and making really good money. So, I kept looking for opportunities to propel this country boy higher.

In time, I got into Electronic Data Systems' business system engineering program boot camp. If the name Electronic Data Systems or EDS sounds familiar, it may be because it's the company Ross Perot started. He was quite an entrepreneur himself starting EDS with a $1,000 investment and turning it into a multi-billion dollar innovative technology services industry leader. Later, he turned to politics when he unsuccessfully ran for president of the United States in 1992 and 1996. The boot camp I went through was a rigorous three-month program where they either make you or break you. Fortunately, I got through it. This afforded me the opportunity to learn business system methodologies and then experience developing and maintaining computer-supported business systems. I was still learning more, but I also knew I was still way down the food chain. Those dreams of advising businesses and making significant money still played in my head. I always had the thought that if someone else could do it then why not me.

So what did I do? I took a flying leap into the technology consulting business. Again, I was stretching myself and gulping water from the fire hose, but most importantly, I was growing and learning—and more than doubling my income. I made sure I was always on top of my game and making my customer happy.

While I was doing this, there was a big company that relocated into town and was going to move from their legacy computer business systems to the latest and greatest ERP (Enterprise Resource Planning) software called SAP (Systems, Applications and Products, a German software company) to run their enterprise-wide business. I was able to be a part of the implementation and got the valuable experience of going through this huge SAP implementation, learning how to do it along the way.

Again, it was time for this country boy to propel himself upward and onward. I took another leap and became a member of a global business consulting firm, multiplying my income again. There I used all my entrepreneurial and survival skills to stretch in a big way to be successful developing, selling, and delivering business consulting services. You definitely have to be entrepreneurial inside a professional services partnership to be successful. You find prospects, understand customers, develop and sell solutions that solve issues and add value, write and negotiate contracts, deliver projects, do joint ventures, develop and manage people, and so much more, such as developing new business methodologies and practices, which I did as a principal (non-CPA partner) in the partnership.

So finally there I was, sitting in elegant conference rooms with senior management consulting on their businesses, privileged to work with some great companies and teams in locations around the world. It was good, but my inner-entrepreneur still wanted to chase and fulfill more dreams.

Ultimately, I leveraged all those years of experience and knowledge in business systems and methods to start my own business information and coaching companies and developed proprietary methodologies and products to enable success for entrepreneurs and businesses.

I have experienced and continue to experience the wide array of challenges that the entrepreneur faces. All the stretching, taking the leaps of risk, hard work—in my view it is completely worth it for that sweet feeling of accomplishment and satisfaction. And if I'm being completely honest, the benefits of success such as a house in a private resort community on a harbor, are nice bonuses, too. I enjoy sitting there looking out through the French doors of my office to the harbor, watching the sailboats pass by, and I think of how success can provide a fortunate lifestyle.

The country boy made it.

## Journey of Rediscovery

Then I got cancer.

In a day, I went from business coach to cancer patient. I vividly remember my doctor lifting his eyes from the report, pushing back from his desk, turning to me and telling me he was sorry but my biopsy results revealed that I have cancer. I remember thinking that this is something that couldn't be happening. There must have been some mistake. I thought that this was something that happens to someone else, not me, but here it was staring me right in the face. Fortunately, we caught the cancer early enough that we were able to deal with it effectively.

Getting diagnosed with cancer readjusted my perspective on life. Somewhere along the way, I had gotten caught up in the pursuit of success, and there's nothing wrong with that, but I had lost some focus on what was truly important in life. My journey now was taking me to where I was a rediscovering soul of those things that I believe and inspire me. I realized that the trappings of success were meaningless without also having what's really important in life. That's being a good husband, father, friend, believer in my Faith, and helper of others. These things are truly my greatest achievements.

During my journey, I also realized anew we only have a certain amount of time on this earth, and we should not put off important goals. Instead, we should invest in ourselves and in others right now.

So I renewed my focus in helping others be successful in reaching the dream goals of their entrepreneurial journey. This is my purpose as founder of my companies that are committed to providing business information and coaching enabling the success of entrepreneurs and businesses. As a businessperson, I understand the issues and challenges that face people and what it takes to succeed. I know that people can exceed their expectations when they are motivated. When someone is motivated and believes in themselves and they combine that with the proper knowledge, planning and execution, they have the ingredients they need to accomplish their goals. They just need a pathway to follow and a way, a bridge, over the challenges.

Through the years of my entrepreneurial journey, I've been privileged to work with some great firms and customers. I've also been humbled by the tremendous results achieved by individuals and teams I've had the opportunity to lead. Now, I'm bringing this knowledge and experience to entrepreneurs and small businesses, which I believe in the past and now again, are the engine of American and global economic progress.

I think nothing is more rewarding than helping people and seeing them reach their goals of success. I've been fortunate to achieve dream goals in my life and have helped others turn their goals or dreams into a reality. If you're ready to further explore your journey as an entrepreneur success story, I want to share in your success with you, by providing you information, motivation, and methods that are proven to work and will help you bridge the barriers to success. We could start with you visiting us at the following website, www.successfulentrepreneuradvisor.com.

# BIBLIOGRAPHY

Adkins, Jasmine D. "Study: Entrepreneurship Programs Continue to Expand." Inc. Magazine. http://www.inc.com/news/articles/200606/colleges.html.

Arrington, Michael. "Internet Entrepreneurs Are Like Professional Athletes, They Peak Around 25." TechCrunch. http://techcrunch.com/2011/04/30/internet-entrepreneurs-are-like-professional-athletes-they-peak-around-25/.

Barrett, Amy. "Case Study: How to Restart a Company." Inc. Magazine. http://www.inc.com/magazine/20110301/case-study-small-business-start-up-financing.html.

Bartlein, Barbara. "The Five Essentials for an Entrepreneur to Start a Business." http://www.career-intelligence.com/transition/Five-Essentials-for-an-Entrepreneur.asp.

Bosma, Niels, and Jonathan Levie. "Global Entrepreneurship Monitor 2009 Global Report." http://www.baf.cuhk.edu.hk/pdf/GEM_Global_2009_Report.pdf.

Branson, Richard. "Richard Branson on the Art of Delegation." Entrepreneur Magazine. http://www.entrepreneur.com/article/219988.

Branson, Richard. "Richard Branson: Finding the Right Balance in Business." Entrepreneur Magazine. http://www.entrepreneur.com/article/217342.

Cole, Bill. "The Fear of Success: How to Overcome It." William B Cole Consultants.

Coulter, Mary. *Entrepreneurship in Action*. N.p.: Prentice Hall, 2002.

Ellis, Blake. "28% of Americans have no emergency savings." CNN. http://money.cnn.com/2012/06/25/pf/emergency-savings/index.htm.

Emmanuel, Matthew. *Methodology Of Business Studies*. Noida, India: Dorling Kindersley, 2010.

Entrepreneur Magazine. "Famous 'Trep Failures -- and Comebacks." http://www.entrepreneur.com/slideshow/219445.

Entrepreneur Magazine. "Startup Financing." http://www.entrepreneur.com/article/52718#.

Ernst & Young. "Nature or Nurture? Decoding the DNA of the entrepreneur." http://www.ey.com/Publication/vwLUAssets/Nature-or-nurture/$FILE/Nature-or-nurture.pdf.

Ewing Marion Kauffman Foundation. "Economic Crisis Survey."
http://www.kauffman.org/uploadedfiles/Econ_Crisis_Survey_9_30_
08.pdf.

Ewing Marion Kauffman Foundation. "Kauffman FastFacts
Entrepreneurship and the Economy."
http://www.kauffman.org/uploadedfiles/factsheet/entrep_and_ec
onomy_fast_facts.pdf.

Fairlie, Robert W. "Kauffman Index of Entrepreneurial Activity
1996-2010." Ewing Marion Kauffman Foundation.
http://www.kauffman.org/uploadedfiles/kiea_2011_report.pdf.

Ferriss, Timothy. *The 4-Hour Work Week*. New York: Crown
Publishers, 2009.

Forbes. "The World's Billionaires."
http://www.forbes.com/billionaires/.

Fritscher, Lisa. "Fears of Failure and Success." About.com.
http://phobias.about.com/od/introductiontophobias/a/fearoffailure.htm.

Godin, Seth. "Engaging with Criticism ."
http://sethgodin.typepad.com/seths_blog/2012/02/engaging-with-
criticism.html.

Gompers, Paul A., Anna Kovner, Josh Lerner, and David S.
Scharfstein. "Performance Persistence in Entrepreneurship."
Harvard Business School.
http://www.hbs.edu/faculty/Publication%20Files/09-028.pdf.

Gongloff, Mark. "Personal Saving Rate Plunges As Americans Get Back To Spending More Than They Earn ." Huffington Post. http://www.huffingtonpost.com/2012/03/30/personal-saving-rate_n_1391333.html.

Greenhouse, Steven. "Starting Over at 55." *The New York Times*, March 3, 2010. http://www.nytimes.com/2010/03/04/business/retirementspecial/04WORK.html.

Hecht, Patricia H. "Individual Psychotherapy - How It Can Help You Overcome Anxiety About Risk Taking." http://ezinearticles.com/?Individual-Psychotherapy---How-It-Can-Help-You-Overcome-Anxiety-About-Risk-Taking&id=6587742

HighBeam Research, Inc. http://www.encyclopedia.com/.

Hill, Napoleon. *Think and Grow Rich*. N.p.: Success Co. Books, 2009.

Howells, Richard. "Why Good Products Fail and What You Can Do About It." Forbes. http://www.forbes.com/sites/sap/2011/07/12/why-good-products-fail-and-what-you-can-do-about-it/.

Kiyosaki, Robert T. *Rich Dad, Poor Dad: What the Rich Teach Their Kids About Money--That the Poor and the Middle Class Do Not!* New York, NY: Warner Books, 2001.

Macmillan Dictionary. http://www.macmillandictionary.com/.

McCorvey, J.J. "The Real Consequences of Office Clutter." Inc. Magazine. http://www.inc.com/articles/2010/01/disorganized-office-space.html.

McCullough, Jill B., and Mary Quist-Newins. "Financial Goals, Concerns and Actions of Women Business Owners." The American College. http://womenscenter.theamericancollege.edu/uploads/documents/Women-Business-Owners-Retirement-Study-022412-v2.pdf.

Mill, John S. *Principles of Political Economy*. Amherst, New York: Prometheus Books, 2004.

Minniti, M, W.D. Bygrave, and E Autio. *Global Entrepreneurship Monitor 2005 Executive Report*. N.p.: Babson College and London Business School, 2005.

Misner, Ivan. "Build Relationships That Last." Entrepreneur Magazine. http://www.entrepreneur.com/article/62140.

Morales, Lymari. "Self-Employed Workers Clock the Most Hours Each Week." Gallup. http://www.gallup.com/poll/122510/self-employed-workers-clock-hours-week.aspx.

Morgan, Nick. "Why We Fear Public Speaking And How To Overcome It." Forbes. http://www.forbes.com/sites/nickmorgan/2011/03/30/why-we-fear-public-speaking-and-how-to-overcome-it/.

Morris, Virginia B., and Kenneth M. Morris. *Dictionary of Financial Terms*. N.p.: Lightbulb Press, 2000.

Mount, Ian. "Why It's Getting Harder, and Riskier, to Bet the House." *New York Times*, November 30, 2011. http://www.nytimes.com/2011/12/01/business/smallbusiness/why-business-owners-routinely-bet-the-house-and-why-its-getting-harder-to-do.html

Pagliery, Jose. "Firms turn to riskier financing." CNN. http://money.cnn.com/2012/02/17/smallbusiness/bank_loans_financing/index.htm.
PBS. "Women & Venture Capital." http://www.pbs.org/ttc/headlines_economics_venture.html.

Politis, Diamanto, and Jonas Gabrielsson. "Prior Career Experience and the Development of Entrepreneurial Knowledge."

Psychology Campus. "Intrinsic Motivation." http://www.psychologycampus.com/sports-psychology/intrinsic-motivation.html.

Quinn, Audra. "Diagram of an Entrepreneur." *Pepperdine Magazine*, July 24, 2009 http://magazine.pepperdine.edu/index.php/2009/07/diagram-of-an-entrepreneur/.

Reinink, Amy. "Entrepreneurship: No Experience Necessary." Entrepreneur Magazine. http://www.entrepreneur.com/article/204508.

Robinson, Joe. "How to Avoid Entrepreneur Overload." Entrepreneur Magazine. http://www.entrepreneur.com/article/219311.

Robinson, Joe. "When Being An Entrepreneur Can Literally Kill You." Business Insider. http://articles.businessinsider.com/2011-04-06/strategy/30082714_1_overwork-stress-finnish-institute.

Rosenberg, Joyce M. "SBA head looks beyond loans to help small business." Business Week. http://www.businessweek.com/ap/2012-05/D9UUKC300.htm.

Schweitzer, Tamara. "Not Only the Lonely Become Entrepreneurs." Inc. Magazine. http://www.inc.com/news/articles/200701/loners.html.

Shane, Scott. " Failure Rates by Sector: The Real Numbers." Small Business Trends. http://smallbiztrends.com/2012/09/failure-rates-by-sector-the-real-numbers.html.

Shane, Scott. " Start Your Business in a Favorable Industry That You Know Well." Small Business Trends. http://smallbiztrends.com/2008/06/start-your-business-favorable-industry-know-well.html.

Stangler, Dane. "The Economic Future Just Happened." Ewing Marion Kauffman Foundation. http://www.kauffman.org/uploadedfiles/the-economic-future-just-happened.pdf.

Staw, Barry M. *Psychological dimensions of organizational behavior*. 3rdrd ed. N.p.: Prentice Hall, 2003.

Success Magazine. "Magic Touch: Magic Johnson's Fast Break Into Business." http://www.success.com/articles/1127-magic-johnson-s-fast-break-into-business.

Sugars, Brad. "The 6 Biggest Mistakes in Raising Startup Capital." Entrepreneur Magazine. http://www.entrepreneur.com/article/184350.

Sullivan, T.A., and J. Westbrook. "Financial Difficulties of Small Business and Reasons for Their Failure." U.S. Small Business Administration. http://archive.sba.gov/advo/research/rs188tot.pdf.

"Television & Health." http://www.csun.edu/science/health/docs/tv&health.html.

The American College. "What Keeps Women Business Owners Up At Night?." http://womenscenter.theamericancollege.edu/assets/pdf/Women BusinessOwnersQuiz.pdf.

*The Small Business Economy December 2008: A Report to the President.* N.p.: U.S. Small Business Administration.

Theil, Stefan. "The Golden Age of Innovation." The Daily Beast. http://www.thedailybeast.com/newsweek/2010/08/20/innovation -grows-among-older-workers.html.

Tice, Carol. "Does College Matter for Entrepreneurs?." Entrepreneur Magazine.
http://www.entrepreneur.com/blog/220306.

Tracy, Brian. "The Four P's of Persuasion."
http://www.briantracy.com/blog/sales-success/the-four-ps-of-persuasion/.

U.S. Small Business Administration. "Business Creation in the United States: Entry, Startup Activities, and the Launch of New Ventures."
http://archive.sba.gov/advo/research/sbe_08_ch07.pdf.

U.S. Small Business Administration. http://www.sba.gov/.

United States Census Bureau. "Business Dynamics Statistics (BDS) Data Tables: Firm Characteristics."
http://www.census.gov/ces/dataproducts/bds/data_firm.html.

United States Census Bureau. "Census Bureau Reports Number of Minority-Owned Firms Increased at More Than Double the Rate of All U.S. Businesses From 2002 to 2007." http://www.census.gov/newsroom/releases/archives/business_ow nership/cb11-103.html.

Vanderkam, Laura. "4 Secrets Happy Entrepreneurs Know." CBS News. http://www.cbsnews.com/8301-505125_162-47240626/4-secrets-happy-entrepreneurs-know/.

Vinturella, John B., and Suzanne M. Erickson. *Raising Entrepreneurial Capital*. Burlington, MA: Butterworth-Heinemann, 2004.

Wadhwa, Vivek, Raj Aggarwal, Krisztina Z. Holly, and Alex Salkever. "The Anatomy of an Entrepreneur: Making of a Successful Entrepreneur." Ewing Marion Kauffman Foundation. http://www.kauffman.org/uploadedfiles/making-of-a-successful-entrepreneur.pdf.

Wellner, Alison S. "Blood Money." *Inc. Magazine*, December 1, 2003 http://www.inc.com/magazine/20031201/gettingstarted.html.

Zwilling, Martin. "The Most Successful People Never Stop Learning Until They Die." Business Insider. http://articles.businessinsider.com/2012-03-11/strategy/31144567_1_big-picture-business-ideas-new-idea.

www.ingramcontent.com/pod-product-compliance
Lightning Source LLC
Chambersburg PA
CBHW060331200326
41519CB00011BA/1905